*"I love my work at Leadership Network (www.leadnet.org) because Of the opportunities I have to meet 100X leaders like Jerry Harris. Guys like Jerry are always thinking about what's next and putting it into practice right now. **Micropolitan Church** is all about how his church, The Crossing, has introduced 'what's next' concepts like multi-site to the small towns of America. Read his book and learn how to think micropolitan and make it work in your community."*

Greg Ligon
Innovator, Pastor, and writer. Greg is the co-author or *Multi-site Church Revolution* and *Multi-site Road Trip*

*"In **Micropolitan Church**, Jerry Harris will strip away the misconceptions and excuses to true discipleship in our communities. His methods will challenge your view of the church, putting it on the attack outside the conventional walls moving people from converts to disciples. Use his team's ideas to implement change in your church without blowing it up. This message could change the direction of the church in America!"*

Jim Putman
Lead Pastor and church planter of Real Life Ministries, One of the largest and most discipleship focused churches in the country. Jim is the author of *Church is a Team Sport* and *Real Life Discipleship*.

Micropolitan Church

Doing Mega-Ministry in America's Small Towns

Jerry Harris

CROSSBOOKS
PUBLISHING

CrossBooks™
A Division of LifeWay
1663 Liberty Drive
Bloomington, IN 47403
www.crossbooks.com
Phone: 1-866-879-0502

First published by CrossBooks 1/27/2011

ISBN: 978-1-6150-7722-9 (sc)
Library of Congress Control Number: 2011921015

Printed in the United States of America

This book is printed on acid-free paper.

Dedication

I dedicate this book to my Lord and Savior Jesus Christ Who gave me the honor and privilege to join Him in His epic work and to my wonderful wife and ministry partner, Allison, who not only said "yes" when I asked her to marry me but has been saying "yes" to ministry ever since.

Jerry Harris

Contents

Introduction

"Well I was born in a small town
And I can breath in a small town
Gonna die in this small town
And that's prob'ly where they'll bury me"

John Mellencamp

I guess you can take the boy out of the small town but you can't take the small town out of the boy. John Mellencamp's tribute to his own life growing up in rural Indiana is contained in many of his songs and they resonate with the heartland of America. So does the story of the great Celtic basketball player Larry Bird who still lives in rural French Lick, Indiana. Mitchell, Indiana hosts a memorial tribute to Virgil "Gus" Grissom, one of the Mercury 7. Gary, Indiana was home to the Jackson 5.

My community in Indiana had a similar feel to it. Although it was really a suburb of Indianapolis, Speedway was self-contained. Our claim to fame was the legendary Indy 500, an event that transformed our little community in the month of May. We had our own fire department, police force, schools, parks, library, and shopping center. My dad was on a first name basis with the grocery store cashier, his barber, the bank teller, and the school superintendent. Many were the same people we would see at the ball game or sit next to at church. It was a great place to grow up. Even though my sisters were as much as 19 years older than me, I had the same teachers so many years later. Sure, there were plenty of people who left Speedway because of college, career, or marriage (I was one of them), but there were plenty who stayed or moved in.

As the years went by, I would often travel back to visit family and friends. The city of Indianapolis sprawled out and eventually swallowed up that peaceful little town. Many things changed but one could always see pieces of an easier time when things made a little more sense, maybe more out of innocence than anything else. That little town had to adjust to the changes around it. Those kinds of changes are happening in small towns all over America. The term "micropolitan" was given to many of these towns by the U.S. Census Bureau. While micropolitan communities are embracing these adjustments, churches have had a difficult time keeping up with their movement.

Like many of you who are reading this, I was comfortable where I was planted in places like Joplin, Missouri, Waynesboro, Virginia, rural Indiana, and now Quincy, Illinois; spending almost all of my professional life in them. They are places that have much of that familiar feeling of home, ranging in size from 1,000 to 40,000. But with limitations of town size coupled with obstacles like tradition, it felt like a lid was on the growth and influence I longed to see. Churches on the cutting edge had all the things I didn't have; money, facility, a talent pool, and a willingness to change. I viewed the books written and models presented by them to be coming from churches and pastors too distant to be adaptable for me. When I came to Quincy, I was determined to blow away those perceived limitations.

Micropolitan Church is a collection of the adapted ideas and the innovative, original thinking that has contributed to a great church impacting the national stage from America's small but micropolitan town. I hope that you would take this book not so much as a template, but as a treasure trove of ideas as you seek to make an everlasting impact in the lives of people... especially God's lost children that He has sent us out to find and bring home.

Part 1: Small Towns Don't Necessarily Mean Small Church

The Crossing's Micropolitan Story

Even before the word was invented, the nation was picking up on the micropolitan phenomena. It was seen a compromise between the benefits of both the urban and rural environments. Quincy, IL is just such a community.

Less than a week before Bill Clinton's final State of the Union address, Quincy officials got word that the President would be coming to town the day after the speech to drive home the agenda for his final year in office. "Why Quincy?" was the initial reaction from many locals. The official White House answer: Quincy's economic recovery and quality of life are prime examples of the economic prosperity the nation has enjoyed in recent years.1

Quincy is an incredibly beautiful town that sits on a bluff overlooking the Mississippi River in west central Illinois. The architecture is magnificent, representing German craftsmanship going back to the mid-1800's. Quincy had made culture and community a high priority as reflected in its art programs and beautiful parks. The downtown district was in the midst of ongoing renovation stemming from the flood of 1993. The atmosphere was friendly and outgoing, yet stable and safe.

My wife and I were being interviewed by the leadership of what was then Payson Road Christian Church. Payson Road was typical….a church that rose and fell somewhere in the 100-300 range in attendance for the past 28 years. Recently, the church had taken some major setbacks. The previous pastor had left under the shadow of immoral behavior. The staff of 4 had shrunk to 1 as a result the indiscretion. The church population also felt the loss of about 100 of its people settling out at about 230. To add insult to injury, the church had just made the decision to go mobile, setting up and tearing down each week at the high school auditorium for services. The bad news broke only a couple of weeks after the major strategic move. Even with the trauma, the church leadership was serious about moving forward.

My wife, Allison, and I had been serving a growing rural church for the last 11 years. Even though the church had tripled in size, I felt a desire to step out of the "business as usual" church for something truly innovative. Although it didn't look like a place where these dreams could become realities from the outside, something was stirring on the inside. There was a sense that these leaders really wanted to be aggressive as an outwardly focused church. They wanted to make a difference. We decided to make the move.

Issues ran deep in the leadership. There were nine people on the leadership team and there were at least four opinions on what direction to go. Some liked the mobile church approach and its outward focus. They wanted to continue in the same model. Since we still owned our church building and shrunk by 100 people, we could go back to our church building and heal. Some wanted this approach. Others wanted to go back to the old building but add on in some way. Finally there were those who wanted to start over and build brand new. These multiple visions were liable to cause lasting divisions. The potential of division was fueled by the open wound of the recent past. Then Tuesday happened….

Only 6 weeks into this new ministry, the weekend looked intimidating. A strategic planning leaders retreat was slated to start on Friday evening. These four directions would come out and some of the leaders had their heels dug in pretty deep. I dropped my kids off at school with the obvious uphill battle on my mind and found myself in a conversation with the school administrator. He mentioned in passing about some modular buildings being for sale at the local community college. I wondered how they might be used if we were to move back to our old facility.

John Wood Community College was centrally located on the east edge of Quincy. It had originally been Lincoln Elementary School, the crown jewel of the Quincy public school system. But the open learning concept it was designed for proved to be ineffective for some students and the building was abandoned along with the concept. JWCC had taken the 22-acre campus over but with 2300 students had outgrown it. They had installed a group of modular buildings to assist in the student expansion but their move to a new campus made them unnecessary. When I began to ask questions about the modulars, a number of suit-clad administrators began to show up and informed me that the entire campus would be for sale. They had plans to build new facilities down the road. It couldn't hurt to ask how much they wanted. The answer was 2.5 million. That number was unthinkable for a small congregation of 230 with no savings. The building could be easily converted but those costs would only add to the already unattainable number.

I went home and asked Allison to drive over to the college with me. We parked in the front, held hands, and prayed that if God wanted us to have this campus, He could make it happen. The administrators had given me some freshly printed brochures designed to sell the campus. I waited for Friday.

After the retreat started, we came to the part about vision and direction. The chairman listed the 4 options that had been previously discussed and one by one we went through them. "I have a 5ᵗʰ option." I told the chairman. The leaders looked at me wondering how there could be another option especially since I was so new to the area and the church. The brochures were passed out as I told the story of what had happened on Tuesday. Something began to happen. In those next 30 minutes, unity electrified the room spreading a new excitement. They believed it could be done…that God could accomplish it. We would have to triple attendance in three years just to manage the payments. This was wonderful, and terrible: both euphoric and terrifying all at the same time.

The congregation embraced the concept. It was amazing to see the change in their faces. The pain of the recent past was replaced with the exhilaration of the future. Negotiations brought an even brighter picture. The property would be purchased at 2.5 million. The college would receive a four times matching grant from the state, 10 million to go with our money for their new campus. They gave us a $250,000.00 credit for our improvements. They agreed to share the building with us as they transitioned to their new campus. We would get 100% of our lease payments applied to our debt. All the furniture they didn't take to the new campus stayed with us. They held our note at their interest rate, a rate substantially lower than the banks. Our old facility sold for $500,000.00 and pledges were raised for over $600,000.00 over a 3-year period. Dr. Bill Simpson, president of the college, when interviewed by the local paper said that the deal we brokered with them was his single greatest contribution as president.

Those events in the fall of 1998 set in motion what was to become a megachurch in Quincy, IL. We wondered how we would ever be able to use 64,000 square feet of building space and 22 acres of land. We didn't have to wonder for long! The church began attracting new families immediately. The newspaper did feature articles on our growth. By 2001, John Wood Community College was in their new facility and we were able to start fully utilizing ours. The children's areas were our first priority. We had built-in observation areas for parents to watch how their children acclimated to their church environment. We knew that un-churched parents wouldn't just blindly trust us. We developed security protocols for child drop off and pick up...not a new idea in metro churches but foreign concepts in a micropolitan. A café at church was also a new idea for our community. Comfortable couches and high tables and chairs invited people to sit down and get to know each other. A bookstore gave churchgoers a place to pick up a DVD of the service or buy a Bible. Student ministries areas were decorated with chain link fencing and graffiti-like painted walls. TV's equipped with X-boxes lined the walls for gamers in the youth area. Students quickly attracted their parents to their new hangout.

Soon, the gym we used as our worship area was holding 4 services on the weekend. We knocked out a wall to hold 200 more seats on the back side of the stage. We used IMAG to provide a good view regardless of which side one sat on.

We realized that the building we thought we could never fill had grown too small. It was then that we added a new auditorium; a pre-engineered steel building capable of seating 2000 people. It was at this point that the community saw our campus as an asset to them for various functions. It gave us great first-impression opportunities. The Crossing began touching 2000 people in weekend attendance, 5% of the community's population of 40,000.

Before we had built the new auditorium, I was researching a sermon series called "Dangerous Church". When I googled it, I found a church based in Oklahoma City called Lifechurch. tv. As I explored the website, I realized that this church was in multiple locations and using technology to connect them. Up to that point, I thought that multi-site strategy wasn't for the smaller towns of the Midwest. People in L.A., Atlanta, or Chicago might be okay with a two-dimensional video preacher, but not west central Illinois! A visit to Lifechurch.tv changed my mind. I remember going to the video experience at their Edmond campus after worship and live preaching at the primary campus in Oklahoma City. I was being surprised at liking the former better. Their south Oklahoma City live video campus was only 6 months old and reaching 2000 a week already!

My team went back to our hotel to talk about it. I said, "We don't know much about church in metropolitan areas, but we know a lot about towns our size." I put forth the question, "Where should we go to reproduce what's happening in Quincy?" Mary Woollard, one of our pastor's wives was attending graduate school at Western Illinois University in Macomb, IL. She said Macomb was a dark place spiritually. It was 60 miles northeast of Quincy. It became our first multi-site location. It had a very interesting texture. The major influence in the community was the university. With 13,000 students in a town of about 20,000, we knew our church's impact could be dramatic. WIU was the community's largest employer. The university made a huge footprint geographically and businesses positioned themselves with it in mind. Most city fathers were WIU graduates as was the planning commission. Like most college towns, there was a lot of partying. As the student body was comprised of about 80% students from the Chicago area, one could sense the frustration with the small town environment, as there was little else to do. The university atmosphere inclined the community to want to embrace new things. The economy wasn't the best as reflected in its micropolitan rating. The population wasn't growing and buildings on the town's main street lay empty. The religious/church culture was a typical micropolitan story. Churches were steeped in traditional mindsets and models at least 50 years old. It was perfect for an outwardly focused church.

We didn't know anyone there and no one there was making the hour-long drive to our church…but we went. We bought a strategically placed grocery store that had been abandoned for 6 years for $750,000.00 and spent another three quarters of a million to rehabilitate it. We loved its location. It was less than half a mile from the university and on the town's main street. The city's planning commission was eager to work with us as they were intent on revitalizing that side of town. They offered help in the rehabilitation and made us welcome. The Crossing was on the front pages of local papers 6 times before we opened. Every day we gave tours of the project for curious residents. There was a buzz all through town about this new church coming to town. We made 12,000 copies of a promotional DVD and mailed them to every home in the area. We also distributed them in the school's dorms. Volunteers from Quincy considered themselves church planting missionaries as they scraped, cleaned, and painted. We hired 5 full-time staff for the new campus.

On October 9, 2007, about 500 people from Quincy joined about 400 total strangers from Macomb to worship. Affordable technology allowed us to broadcast the sermon live from Quincy. Everything else was local. The enthusiasm was deafening. Two years later, the Crossing Macomb is running just under 1000 people reflecting nearly 5% of their micropolitan community, and 80% of those who attend have little or no church background. Standing on it's own feet financially, the Crossing Macomb is making a dramatic impact as the largest church in the community.

Jerry Harris

Even before launch day at Macomb, a small group of people in Kirksville, MO had heard about what we were doing. About 60 of them started driving weekly the hour and a half drive to Quincy to worship with us. They asked us to consider repeating Macomb's experience in Kirksville. Our elders didn't want to talk to them. We felt like our hands were full, but the victories were too awesome to ignore. Once again we went. We were able to purchase what had been a shoe factory on the south side of town for $500,000.00. It was a 106,000 square ft. building on 19 acres of property. Once again we hired a 5 full-time staff. Once again, we were regulars on radio, television, and newspapers. When we launched in Kirksville, nearly 500 people from town were there! Today, Kirksville has held those numbers continuing as the largest church in their area. Just over a year old at this writing, they are over doing what would have been considered impossible with cutting edge technology.

In 2008, the Crossing went international, establishing a multi-site in Mosselbay, South Africa. Crossing sermon vodcasts are downloaded from itunes and used along with live worship. More than two hundred share services with us. The Crossing at Mosselbay is the only integrated church in the area, breaking through age-old racist barriers. Plans are in the works to partner with an existing church in Chennai, India. Both locations appeal to us as their location is on the southern tips of two continents...truly the ends of the earth.

Also in 2008, the Crossing began a process of opening thrift stores in all their locations. The stores multiplied benevolence given exponentially. They have provided jobs for the communities and put much needed resources in the hands of those who need them at very low prices. The addition of both human and financial resources brought benevolence more into focus as a bridge to people in need.

In January 2010, the Crossing launched the Crossing 929, an inner-city extension campus in Quincy for the purpose of bringing people into an intimate, personal relationship with Christ through benevolence ministry. We were able to raise all the necessary funds for the new work in a single offering, making 929 debt free from its birth.

As the Crossing looks to the future, we continue to have a "If you can dream it, you can do it!" mentality. In communities that others would consider stagnant, the Crossing has been defining a new paradigm: the micropolitan church. Hundreds of people have come to Christ and the church looks to its next micropolitan multi-site location in a geographic area that reaches people 165 miles wide regionally and stretches to the very ends of the earth.

What is micropolitan?

A) a frozen dessert at TCBY;
B) a popular magazine for young short women;
C) a metro area in miniature.

If you answered C, the U.S. Census Bureau would like to shake your hand.2 "Micropolitan" is a label the Bureau created in 2003 to describe population centers from 10,000 and 50,000 that fill the gaps on the map between major cities. They serve as a new way of looking at rural America and where it's headed. That direction is something that observers are still figuring out. It's not yet clear whether they represent a new urban environment rising up from small towns or an improved rural America version.

There are approximately 577 micropolitan communities in the United States. One in ten Americans call a micropolitan community home. Their existence and growth reflect a culture longing for something a little less metro; without the insanity of traffic, with better schools, familiar faces, and easier community connections. At the same time, they offer amenities that metro areas used to hold exclusively like the Lowe's Home Improvement Store, Applebee's, and of course, Wal-Mart. They have become hubs for rural people to shop, eat, get medical attention, or go to community college.

Policom research firm ranks these communities using 23 types of data, including the number of jobs in a community, personal income, retail sales, construction figures and welfare levels. In the 3 stateside areas where the Crossing ministers, the ranking varies greatly. Quincy, IL ranks at #158. Macomb, IL on the other hand is #547, just 30 from the bottom. Kirksville,

MO is #494. Regardless of ranking or demographics, each community has a fingerprint all its own.

Inside that fingerprint remains a virtually undiscovered potential to grow cutting-edge churches that can influence whole regions for Jesus Christ. Although micropolitan communities have their limitations, their strengths can easily outweigh them. It's those strengths that can be exploited for the growth of the kingdom of God and give the church access to the 30 million people living in them that long for something that works for them spiritually.

Micropolitan communities are anything but typical. In Colorado, they might be getaway enclaves for upscale families built around recreation. In Arizona or Florida they might be retirement communities. Winchester, Virginia was a small town of 20,000 in 1980. D.J. Chuang wrote, "Nothing to do except cruising and the purist medium vanilla cone at Pack's Frozen Custard. Today, there is a new Starbucks just east of I-81. It sits amidst a giant strip mall with dozens of franchise stores. All the big brands are here now: Borders, Olive Garden, Circuit City, Five Guys, Maggie Moo, Target, Outback Steakhouse, Red Lobster, Lowe's, Home Depot, Quizno's, and Red Hot & Blue. Of course, Wal-Mart has been here for years." **3**

Jack Schultz recently wrote *Boomtown USA: The 71/2 Keys to Big Business in Small Towns.* As the head of Agracel, an industrial development company based in Effingham, IL, Schultz recruits manufacturing and high-tech businesses to small towns he calls "agurbs." He did it in his hometown of Effingham, a micropolitan area of more than 34,000 people. When the city lost major manufacturers, Schultz led an effort to build the 1.43 mile Effingham Railroad to create a connection with two major rail lines. As a result, Krispy Kreme came to town. "We're too small to have a Krispy Kreme store, but we've got their national manufacturing facility." Schultz says.

"People from large cities have the stereotype of small towns as being backward and not offering any advantages." I think the advantages are plenty. Cheaper land, cheaper construction, lower labor rates, and a small-town quality of life.4 On the Thomasville-Lexington, NC micropolitan community he writes, "The message coming out of both this community and Statesville-Mooresville is that both succeeded in the long run because they developed a strong manufacturing base. Companies feel comfortable going there because of the strong work ethic. But communities have to continually reinvent themselves. You can't rest on your laurels … You always have to proceed as though you are on the bottom of the heap."

Jack's advice needs to be taken seriously by the church. The laurels many churches are resting on have gotten pretty old. Like communities, churches that want to make a difference have to constantly reinvent themselves as well. A Micropolitan community is a great place to do just that.5

Colleen Pepper of *Leadership Network* writes, "Given the prominence of churches like these, one might assume that the shift to multi-campus churches is happening only in suburban areas. However, more than a third of survey respondents were from churches located outside the suburbs, including small towns, rural areas, and urban centers. Even more interesting, the survey suggests that churches in these areas may enjoy greater fruit. Respondents from suburban churches with four or more campuses reported an average of 141% growth since first going multi-site—compared with 202% growth at urban multi-site churches, and a jaw dropping 412% at small town/ rural multi-site churches."6 This is good evidence that the percentages are stacked in the favor of micropolitans.

98% of churches are not "mega", or located in an area where most "mega" models don't quite fit. However, we keep buying books that discuss their models. The micropolitan church is a model for the rest of us...churches who are sold out to do whatever it takes to make a difference right where we're planted. So, from the heart of the Midwest, here are the steps we took to become that micropolitan church, some pitfalls to watch out for, and the benefits of taking the risks.

What is a Micropolitan Church?

A micropolitan church is much more than a church existing in a micropolitan community. It's a church doing the same thing the community is doing, taking the great attributes only once afforded by metropolitan or suburban churches and marrying them to the micropolitan environment. It's a church recognizing its incredible potential because of its location and leveraging its resources to make that potential into a reality.

What's so special about a micropolitan church? It's their environment that makes them unique. They really aren't doing anything much different than any other growing church. Relevant teaching, progressive worship, deep discipleship, and cutting edge technology are not new concepts. It's *where they are* that makes *what they are* special. Maybe it comes from asking the question, *"Why not?"*. *Why not* do what metropolitan churches are doing? Why not be a megachurch in a small community? *Why not* be casual when everybody else is traditional? *Why not* branch out into multi-sites from one micropolitan to another? *Why not* step out in extreme faith and make a huge investment a distant community?

Maybe they've become churches that don't know their place. There are certain expectations for churches in micropolitan communities. They are expected to be the "Bob Evans" of churches. You know, "The way it was is the way it is." These communities expect sunrise services followed by pancake breakfasts. They expect hanging of the greens at Christmas. They expect church fans on hot days, carry-in dinners, and communion in glass cups. They expect the olive green carpet and those sanctuary lights that look like giant hanging ashtrays. They expect the old lady playing the electric organ, the wooden board with the attendance numbers, and the doxology sung after the offering is collected. You get the picture.

We are what you don't expect...not here anyway. We're the church where people come as they are, where kids play halo 3 in the student area, where the programs have no order of worship in them. We're the church that helps someone recover from their meth addiction while teaching him to run a camera for worship services. We're the church that realizes that wearing jeans with holes in them doesn't mean they're worn out. We're the church that understands that coffee can be served in more ways than with just cream or sugar.

Who are Micropolitan People?

There is a reason why people live where they do. A lot of it has to do with occupation. Some of it has to do with preference. For many, it is simply all they've ever known and they're comfortable with it. It is absolutely key to get underneath the surface of a community to understand what its needs are. Micropolitan churches have to establish a laser focus on targeting. Demographics only go so far in answering this question. Hearing the stories of people in the community, how they got there, what they're motivation is in staying, and their plans for the future give a "feel" or texture for the community.

The stories below are illustrations of how people find themselves in micropolitan communities and a micropolitan church. For those who live in them, a progressive and attractive church is a rarity. *Most micropolitan communities have plenty of churches in them. What they don't have is a church that takes an aggressive stance to reach the 80+% of people in those communities who don't or won't go to church.*

---

(1)

Brad and Jessi are being moved by a company called Gardner Denver to their corporate offices in Quincy, IL. Brad's career is taking a big leap forward as head of human resources. The rest of the family has a different take on the situation. Their 14 year-old daughter Abby loves her dance troupe and is rebelling against leaving it along with losing all her friends. Jessi has her career in pre-school education and her social group. Brad is definitely facing an uphill battle. Quincy has little to offer for a family comfortable in suburban Atlanta.

The move is about 9 months old when Brad is having lunch with Bryan, one of the company's marketing directors. After some surface conversation about the weather and football scores, Bryan asks how Brad's family has been handling the move. Brad puts up a good front at first, but slowly the dam breaks. It's been a tough transition. Jessi isn't complaining but he can see how she misses her relationships. He can feel the distance between them growing and he's worried. Bryan invites Brad to a small group Bible study they have in their home. Brad's defenses go up reflexively. When Bryan tells him that they go to The Crossing it rings a bell with Brad. That's the church where their daughter Abby has been going. Her new friends at school invited her to *Studio 16*. It has become her oasis in the desert. He thinks about finding a place where his family can come together again.

When he throws out the idea to the family, Abby lights up. Both Brad and Jessi have some pre-conceived notions about church involving slick-haired preachers and women with platinum hair and too much makeup sitting in golden chairs asking for money. Their first Sunday is a shock. The building doesn't even look like a church. The parking lot is packed but a parking attendant helps them find a place and greets them. They notice the people are relaxed and wearing comfortable clothes. They pass a place that looks like Starbucks and Jessi grabs a designer coffee for 3 bucks. The worship experience really sets them back. The room looks more like a theater than a church. The chairs are comfortable. The music is contemporary with a leader in ripped jeans singing against a backdrop of haze, intelligent lighting, and video. The sermon is practical yet moving. Brad looks over to Jessi and squeezes her hand. This wasn't expected. Abby hides a big smile. Questions are forming in Brad's head to ask Bryan.

(2)

There is a job opening at Pella Windows in Macomb, IL. For Ben and Allison, the move from Chicago is a big one. The pay is pretty good but the cost of living is only a fraction of what they are presently paying. The university is close by allowing Allison to finish her schooling. They can easily buy twice the house and they're only a $25 Amtrak ticket from all their friends. The thought of reclaiming the 90 minutes a day that Ben spends in his car going to and from work is a very pleasant thought. They're both convinced that it would be a great place to put down roots and raise a family. The down side is that there isn't much in the way of entertainment. There is little in the way of theater, good movies, restaurant choices, shopping, and culture…at least compared to Chicago.

The tour of Macomb doesn't take long…just a short drive down Jackson Street and you've seen a lot of it. Close to the University campus they pass what looks like a store with a big red and black sign that says The Crossing. "That's where we go to church," says the Pella rep. "You need to give it a try. I wasn't a church person, but that place is different." Allison thinks that it would be a perfect place to build some relationships as they attended a church off and on in Chicago.

Their first Sunday wasn't what they expected either. The technology reminded them of home. They could hardly believe that there would be a church like this in Macomb, IL. Allison stopped by the *connecting point* to get information about a small group. Ben asked about the thrift store next door. The guy at connecting point said that 100% of the money from the thrift store went for benevolence in the community. That impressed Ben. The down side of their expectations just went back up a few notches. They thought about a little one playing in the play place. This place could really fill in the gaps.

(3)

Joey was born and raised in Kirksville, MO. It's been a good fit. He loves being an assistant coach for the high school football team. He's dating a girl who goes to Truman State University in town. He's renting a little bungalow close to the college. His parents and younger sister live where they always have across town. "Across town" is only a 10-minute drive. His first love is guitar but he's never really had an outlet for his passion. Kaitlyn, his girlfriend goes to the campus ministry sometimes but it really didn't trip Joey's trigger.

A church called The Crossing bought the shoe factory up on the hill on the south side of town. Everybody's talking about it. The shoe factory has been closed for seven years and how could a church ever use all that space. People are wondering if they are a cult. It's big news for a town like Kirksville and the curiosity is more than a person can take. Certainly it can't hurt to check it out...just don't drink the kool-aid.

There was no way Joey was going alone. Kaitlyn would know better how to handle this kind of place and would run interference if someone tried to "convert" him. Although he liked what he saw when he walked in, it was what he heard that really captured him. The leader on the stage was shredding a vintage Gibson and it was...well...like butter! A couple of his friends caught his eye and before he knew it, they were taking him to the worship leader to talk about playing. Kaitlyn was content to stand back and laugh to herself at God's ability to find the one place in Joey's heart that was vulnerable. Now Joey leads a prayer before the team goes out to play and you can find him bending the "e-string" at worship on Sundays.

In our area of the country this is typical. While metropolitan and suburban areas have megachurches competing for churchgoers, micropolitan communities tend to be places where churches with the attributes of megachurches are hard to find. The result is for those who move into those communities to settle for what is there or to quit going. Those who already live in those communities aren't motivated to make a major life change to get involved in the same old same old. Even more alarming are the number of people who have made the attempt to integrate into a church only to be hurt by things that range from petty issues to child molestation. *Our studies showed that the ratio of churched to un-churched reflect a sad truth...less than 20% attending church, and even that number is shrinking.*

The church growth movement is just beginning in the micropolitan community and the potential for the Kingdom of God is more than we can imagine! When churches in micropolitan communities get serious about reaching the 80% of the people in their community who are un-churched or under-churched, all sorts of opportunities open for them.

Who can use Micropolitan Church?

The obvious targets of this book are those churches that already exist in the 577 micropolitan communities. By using and adapting ideas and models from churches like the Crossing, these churches can become evangelical powerhouses developing formerly unchurched people into excited and committed disciple-makers. There is an ebb and flow to America's population. At this point, urbanization is "generally" where the culture is moving. I emphasize "generally" because we have missed the millions who aren't longing for urban lifestyle. Church growth experts and church planters are concentrating their efforts on following that "general" subset of the population. However, 10% of the population are staying put. The cultural pendulum will be swinging back as it always does, probably in favor of less urban environments in the future. Micropolitan churches will be ready. In the mean time, there is plenty of opportunity right in front of us.

But is the focus of this book too narrow? Is there just not enough market for this new paradigm? I don't think anything could be further from the truth! Metropolitan communities can benefit from it as well. I was talking to Todd Hudson, senior pastor of Southeast Christian Church in Parker, Colorado. Southeast is a church of over 4,000 located just outside the loop around Denver. Because it is technically associated with Denver as suburban, Parker is not considered micropolitan. However, in talking to Todd about The Crossing multi-site approach, Todd started thinking of all the communities around Parker that he would have access to. While those communities may be different than Parker, a micropolitan approach coupled with multi-site would give access to them based out of a healthy and vibrant metropolitan megachurch. Steve Gillen, multi-site director and campus pastor at Willow Creek told me that they were looking for a fresh model for those communities around west central Chicagoland as people were struggling to get to their South Barrington campus. Steve knew Kirksville because it was where he went to college. Hearing about our success there encouraged him to look more closely at adapting the micropolitan model for areas surrounding Willow Creek.

Let's not stop there. I spent 11 years ministering in a rural community of 900 people. I frequently attended conferences and seminars featuring mega-church speakers from metropolitan communities. It was more disheartening than encouraging. The gap between where they were and where I ministered was just too wide. They had big budgets, big talent, big everything. It just wasn't adaptable to where I was working. Jim Putman, senior pastor at Real Life Ministries in Post Falls, Idaho, relates similar feelings at the beginning of his ministry in his book, *Church is a Team Sport*. Since he couldn't do what he saw at a successful mega-church, it forced him to ask, "What can I do well?" That question and the journey to find the answer propelled Jim and Real Life Ministries to be one of the fastest growing and successful churches in the country, with attendance approaching 9000! Why do I tell you this? Post Falls, Idaho is a micropolitan community of 40,000. That means nearly 1 out of every 4 people in that area attend Real Life. Rural churches find it difficult to connect with success models of metropolitan mega-churches because their approach is just not adaptable. *Micropolitan Church* is showing them a model a lot closer to where they are. It's not nearly as big a leap to look at a model provided by a church located in a community of 10,000-50,000 if you minister in a community of less than 10,000.

So what am I saying? I think that almost any church in any setting can use this model. The benefits are awesome.

What are the Benefits of Being Micropolitan?

1. **The most profound benefit of a cutting-edge micropolitan church is its influence on the community.** Even a monster megachurch of 20,000 has only a marginal influence in a metropolitan area. They go virtually unnoticed by the prevailing culture most of the time. Not so with a micropolitan megachurch. They not only have an influence, they are community shapers.

It was truly an eye-opening experience to walk into a McDonald's and notice that out of the 40 eating there, 2 or 3 would be from our church. It is that way everywhere in town because our church population is such a large subset of the population as a whole. There are so many doors that open in a community when the church makes such a large footprint. While distance grows between the micropolitan church and other community churches, it narrows with regards to the target area of the 80% who don't attend anywhere. Our church is now featured in the visitor's guide of Quincy visitors bureau. They see us as an asset to the community. The police department trains in our building, the emergency management agency uses us for a shelter, the high school uses our facility for graduation, and the largest dance academy does its recitals here. The local bank did a full page spread highlighting the Macomb staff for banking with them.

Each door we walk through exposes more people to our unexpected atmosphere. We have access to the mayor's office, the community college president's office, the sheriff, the chief of police, and the head of the planning commission. Because smaller communities are tighter knit, who you know is often much more important than what you know. Since our desire is to impact who we know in the community, those open doors make all the difference. One definition for leadership is taking people to a place they would have never gone by themselves. In a micropolitan community, a church like this will get noticed. It will be noticed by the 80% who have disregarded the church. It will be noticed by the other churches and not appreciated. We have often heard words like "cult" or "shallow" associated with our approach. It almost exclusively comes from the traditional church community...not the 80%. Since our desire is to reach the un-churched and under-churched, we disregard it. It won't be a fit for everybody, but it is amazing to see how many do find their way in.

2. **Most well-used ideas in metropolitan areas are totally fresh in micropolitans. Resources from proven programs are plentiful.** Technologies once out of reach are now easily affordable and much more user friendly. The disparity between a technologically informed church and a typical traditional church is breathtaking. It communicates that the church is in touch with the culture as these tools are used in the workplace. The community will connect the dots between technological relevance and the church understanding where they are.

Solomon told us that there is nothing new under the sun. It has always been so beneficial to benchmark cutting-edge churches in metropolitan and suburban areas in order to glean ideas that can be adapted to use in our setting. While we have found that these churches are rarely frugal when it comes to innovation, our creative team has figured out ways to adapt it to make it work. Our first projection screens were canvas drop cloths stretched over a home made wood frame. We saw a circular screen once and duplicated it by getting a used yard trampoline and painting the bouncing surface with white projection paint. We built a 54-foot wide waterfall on stage with 2x4 framing, drop cloths, pvc pipe, and 2 sump pumps.

These innovative ideas are all around in video technology, lighting, aesthetics, curriculum, and software, even buildings. Being a step or two behind the latest thing in a megachurch is way out front in a micropolitan area. When we saw the children's areas at Lifechurch.tv in Oklahoma City, we had to pray about our coveting. Their wall murals had a Disney world feel. Someone on our staff knew someone in South Africa who had the ability to paint with the same expertise. We flew him over for about a month and for a fraction of the cost, had an environment every bit as awesome. We also saw their church's computerized check-in system for children. We knew that would make un-churched families feel much more secure about dropping off their children. None of the small churches in our community do anything like this. They trust each other because they all know each other. This isn't true with the unchurched 80%...we have to establish trust and that takes time. But when a child is picked up crying because they have to leave, the mission has been accomplished.

The local McDonald's had a child hurt in their play place. They chose to remove the attraction and since we have church people that work at the restaurant, we heard about it. We offered to write a tax exemption letter for it and the labor to remove it. Now church kids play in it. Wendy's decided to remodel and didn't want their salad bar. We got that too. Western Illinois University decided to update their lobby furniture. We bought 71 overstuffed lobby chairs for $1 each. The point is that as doors open up opportunities for this style of church and ideas rush in from church benchmarking, awesome things can happen for very little or no money. Traditional churches would struggle with play places, ball pits, salad bars, and such.

Watching these ideas become realities, other staff members will be filled with ideas to transform certain areas of the building. Although there is a difference between the ultra-professional look of these megachurches and what we have, there is no competition in our micropolitan area.

3. **Micropolitan churches target the unaffected and disconnected.** They are appealing to those hurt in a previous church experience as they see this church as something different. The majority of micropolitan populations are not "connected". They are not part of the country club or the old money in the community. They are looking for a place they can fit in. While the cultural establishment may not know how to take the micropolitan church, those who find it, love it.

I once heard a commercial on a Christian radio station for a local church. The ad said that if you were looking to join a church with "stable" families, you should try theirs. I still remember how that word hit me. If there is one thing the ministry has taught me, families and individuals are truly seldom stable. The Crossing wants the unstable. We want the sick to find the Physician, the broken to find the Carpenter, the ruined to find the Counselor and we are serious about it.

All of our campuses have a Celebrate Recovery program. People that represent those programs are at every service to hook up with people who might need a friend or familiar face. Each campus has a thrift store to provide inexpensive solutions for those in need. If they can't afford anything, we write them a voucher for their needs. We take the time to counsel with them and help them into a small group. 100% of the money received in our thrift stores goes to local benevolence. All three stores generate almost a quarter of a million dollars after expenses per year to help people in the communities. Each store employs about 7 full and part time employees who need jobs. It also gives a different way for our church to give besides money in the collection plate. This missional approach gets our people involved in community for Christ and opens their eyes to its needs.

The micropolitan church is also a great place to build connections with others. Most churches do things the way they've always done. It's safe and predictable. They know what's coming next in the service, the words to the songs, and the faces of the people around them. The 80% don't know where to go, what to do, or who the people are. The micropolitan church puts them at ease before they park their car. There is constant reinforcement around every corner and through every door. They feel welcome and appreciated, not like an intruder. I've seen churches ask visitors to stand up in the service, who give guests no space or anonymity. We take the comfort away from the regular attender. There is no order of worship, the songs change regularly, and no one knows what to expect. We are always thinking of ways to level the playing field. Megachurches figured this out long ago, but churches in micropolitans haven't. It is an incredible opportunity.

4. **Micropolitan communities often are economically depressed so buildings and land are financially attainable at bargain prices.** The church can revitalize a vacant building and bring new beauty to the community. Plus, planning commissions are favorably inclined to churches pumping cash into a depressed economy.

When the Crossing purchased the John Wood Community college campus, it was a turning point. The community noticed it. Even though it was a prime location, the building was just to large and odd for many uses. It was going to be difficult to sell. They were very motivated to work with us, providing shared space, a lease to purchase, our financing, and even furniture.

When the Crossing stretched out 60 miles northeast to Macomb, we quickly found an empty 56,000 sq. ft. building once used as a grocery store. It was on Macomb's main street and very close to Western Illinois University. It had 300 parking places and 6 acres of property. It had been on the market 6 years in the depressed community with no takers. We purchased it for $750,000.00. That's $13.40 per sq, ft. not including the land or parking. We spent another $750,000.00 on making a church out of it. That's a cutting edge church in Macomb for less than $27 bucks a foot!

In Kirksville, we found an empty shoe factory sitting atop a hill south of town on 19 beautiful acres of land. The building was 104,000 sq. ft., lots more than we needed. It also had more than 300 parking places. It had been sitting empty for 8 years. We were able to purchase it for $500,000.00. We gave a tax break to the owner against its appraised value to get it for that price. That was less than $5 per foot. We spent just under a million dollars rehabilitating it. Once again, we had a cutting edge building for very little money. Both Macomb and Kirksville had plenty of room left over for our thrift stores.

Both communities were happy to work with us to revitalize these properties, streamlining regulations and giving us breaks. We were able to use local contractors for much of the work, pumping money into the local economy. While metropolitan or suburban areas require astronomical prices for used buildings or property, and new construction on purchased property can easily cost over $200 per foot, micropolitan properties are a wellspring of opportunity. They also have substantially less red tape. Micropolitan communities are much more likely to take seriously a church that is willing to make such a substantial investment in their area. At the very least, it will make them curious.

5. **Micropolitan church buildings can provide a much-needed facility for community functions.** It is maybe the largest, most technologically advanced, and comfortable venue in the community. People will want to use it for

dance recitals, concerts, and other functions. This gives the church a built-in edge on first impressions. Micropolitan communities often have holes that the church can fill using the arts, music, and culture.

The first time we tried to find a place to meet in Macomb to introduce the community to our vision, we had a difficult time just finding a place to meet. Before we purchased, we tried to find rental space but were shut out. What we learned from this was the absence of good community meeting areas, especially larger settings. Even if there were something, any technology would be non-existent. We saw an incredible opportunity here. When storms or other natural disasters have come through, the Crossing has taken an aggressive approach to meet those needs. Empty space in Kirksville has been used to store furniture after a tornado hit the town and surrounding areas. Parking lots have served as staging areas for power companies to get power back on. Church volunteers serve food and provide shelter for people in need.

Two of our locations have held "Taste of Home" experiences. Other churches have even used our facilities as their bolted down furniture and traditional environment won't lend itself to some functions. We have held seminars for insurance and investment agencies and brokers. They have been used for all sorts of community functions. We have the benefit of our rental rates and at the same time get the exposure of our church facilities to some people who might have never darkened the door otherwise. One local dance academy was so thrilled with our technology and our helpful technicians that they offered to purchase additional equipment that we could keep so they could use it for their recitals.

Once again, we have found common ground with our communities. They have a favorable attitude toward us considering us to be a willing part of the fabric of the community. They are taken by surprise because what they see inside our building doesn't fit their pre-conceived notion of what a church should look like.

6. **Micropolitan churches get plenty of free media attention.** Micropolitan communities are limited in the exciting and new things that are happening in their communities. There is plenty of free advertising that comes from a curious newspaper or television station. Word of mouth travels faster in micropolitans as connections are closer. The power of invitation is greatly magnified.

As we were negotiating with the community college in Quincy for the purchase of their land, it was big news. We had multiple interviews with local television stations and were on the front page multiple times. We are frequently contacted to give a church based opinion about a current event. When our Macomb location was under construction, we were on the front pages of local papers 6 times before we ever opened. We stationed volunteers at the church to give curious community members tours of the building. They were encouraged to ask questions. Word of mouth travels fast across a small town. So much of the media cost just to get noticed in a metropolitan community is just not necessary in a micropolitan. Excitement and curiosity for the project and the church to follow is built in.

7. **Micropolitan churches can make a big splash very quickly.** If they break far enough away from the pack of traditional churches, they will quickly stand alone as the church for the 80%. What is more, the micropolitan church will hold a monopoly on their new position. Tradition has overwhelming inertia. Most traditional churches require great amounts of time to even change small things. Since American culture is reinventing itself every two years, traditional churches can't or won't catch up.

Macomb launched with nearly 900 people on their first Sunday. Probably around 500 of them were from Quincy. As the Quincy people began to tail off, Macomb bottomed out at about 450. Their growth continued back to 800 in less than 18 months. The fact is that the Crossing launched as the largest church in the area on their first Sunday and continue to be the largest church with the biggest community influence to this day. Where else in the United States does this happen? Where else in America can so much be accomplished for so little comparatively?

Recently, I attended a meeting of a church-planting group in Bolingbrook, Illinois. They were looking for some of the large churches in the state to make a big investment in the south loop of Chicago. They talked about the needs of the metro area and the requirements it would take to establish a church to service it. I remember the organizer stating that if they could run 200 in three years, it would be an awesome success. They went around the table to see who would support the work financially. I already had a bigger yes. For the money they were going to spend, I could put micropolitan churches in 4 communities and have them running 500 each from day one. The decision wasn't hard for me. While I think it would be great to have another church in Chicago and that it might be more glamorous, a micropolitan community is a more fertile field…still going unnoticed.

Kirksville launched a year after that meeting with almost 600 in attendance. After 6 months, they are also bottoming out at about 400 and I have no doubt that they will be running 600 in a year. They too are the largest church in their area from day one. This phenomenal establishment and growth is happening in areas that remain overlooked. Megachurch minded people like living in metropolitan areas but those who are hungry to really make a difference and do it quickly need to take a fresh look at a well 30 million people deep.

31

Jerry Harris

Inability to move and move quickly seems to be built in to many churches. By-laws and board meetings trump an aggressive approach. There are just too many obstacles to change to get anything substantial done. This is especially prevalent in micropolitan communities. I bring this up because a micropolitan church will be too hard for many other churches to imitate. There has to be a special chemistry for it to work.

8. **A micropolitan church is a reproducible model.** It can be transplanted with multi-site technology to other micropolitan locations in the region. Soon, a micropolitan church can claim an entire region as its own. While metropolitan areas might tire of franchises like Starbucks, micropolitan communities love a new franchise coming to town. It legitimizes the area as an "arrival" for them.

Today's technology and the acceptance and use of that technology in every other area of society has opened incredible doors for the church. Not only is it available, its affordable. I remember when churches first started going to multiple services. It was resisted because there was a feeling that the church family would be split apart, each service developing its own personality. Resistance eventually gave way to acceptance to those who wanted to maximize their facilities. The church growth movement ran parallel to ideas like that. It lifted a lid to growth as churches transcended time.

The multi-site movement is very similar. Instead of transcending time, we transcend space. Through multi-site technology, we can be more than one place at the same time. Conventionally, it has been used for multiple venues within the same location or targeting a group who drives to church from a different part of town and putting a venue there.

The micropolitan model coupled with multi-site is an exponential leap. It represents a regional approach to doing ministry and can blanket a huge area. Now, in our vision discussions, we talk about which time zone people are in. While many multi-sites choose to use a recorded technology, the Crossing does most of its services live. We do that because we feel that there is real value in doing church in a live format at the multi-site. It makes the multi-site venue feel truly connected. And as it will be discussed later, it is really affordable and relatively easy to do live.

So much of what the Crossing does is exportable. We pre-produce all the materials that our other venues need for early childhood, children, and students. Everything they need for teaching, crafts, music, and small groups is packaged and boxed. Everything is there to make a volunteer an incredible leader. We share resources and staff as well. It makes for much better use of our resources for maximum impact. So many things that work well don't need to be reinvented. Staff and leaders understand they are part of something making a major difference in a large area. There is plenty of coaching and cooperation available. We have discovered that the scripture, "A cord of three strands is not easily broken," applies to churches as well as individuals.

9. **Micropolitan churches are evangelistic magnets.** Progressive worship, relevant teaching, great children experiences, and the edgy atmosphere are very attractive to the un-churched. People feel comfortable in an atmosphere where everyone is new. Micropolitans are virtually untapped evangelistically with most modern and post-modern methods. Be prepared for giving to be much lower but victories to be much higher. You will be flooded with stories of transformation as Jesus does His work. Transfer growth from other churches usually consist of those who share that evangelistic vision and are frustrated because they have no outlet for it.

Since the church is targeting the 80%, that's who comes. The micropolitan church has found a tremendous need in the community, a deep well to draw from, and stands alone to reap the benefit. It works from all of the benefits of being micropolitan because it's where it is that makes what it is special.

Part 2: How To Think Micropolitan

The Micropolitan church focuses it's efforts in five areas. None of these areas are new but the way they look in a micropolitan setting needs to be understood. Each one is critical to the DNA of what this model is all about. It's these five components that make our unique spiritual DNA at The Crossing.

Think Leadership

One of my favorite Bible verses of church leadership is
Psalm 78:71-72:
"He chose David his servant and took him from the sheep pens
From tending the sheep he brought him to be
the shepherd of his people Jacob, of Israel his inheritance.
And David shepherded them with integrity of heart;
With skillful hands he led them."

These verses couple the two most important concepts pastor must possess; leadership and humility. Humble leadership is an oxymoron of sorts. It takes a certain amount of pride and arrogance to believe that you would even possess a worthy vision, let alone seek to impose it on others to see it carried out. These verses point out that David's calling really never changed, he just shepherded a different flock of sheep! Moving from the shepherd's fields to a palace in Jerusalem was only a backdrop for the same responsibility. The lions and bears were replaced with invading armies and internal uprisings, but David's job was still to watch over and protect the sheep. Dancing before the Lord with all of his might as the Ark of the Covenant approached Jerusalem, David chose humility instead of pomp and circumstance. David's attitude was critical for maintaining humility while leading, especially in times of success.

The second part of the text refers to the two most important tools required to be a leader worth following; a heart of integrity and skillful hands. For a leader, these two attributes cannot be allowed to exist apart from each other. We all know some incredibly skillful leaders that could preach, teach, cast vision, raise money, and motivate people only to have imploded because of integrity problems. Let's not forget the person these verses are talking about. No one could dispute the fact that David was a leader with skills. He was incredible at decision-making, strategy, confidence building, loyalty, surrounding himself with other great leaders, and wisdom. But his failure with Bathsheba set a course for his life that cancelled much of his greatness out. Isn't it amazing how much skill can be cancelled out by just one major failure? That is the nature of integrity; it generates so much strength but in itself is only as strong as the first big failure. I know some pastors with great character but very little in the way of skill. People may admire them but would be hard pressed to follow them into the dangerous waters of change or opposition.

Micropolitan communities need great leaders defined by these two qualities of skill and integrity. Humility builds a perfect foundation for integrity. It seems that when we get a high opinion of ourselves, believing our own press, that we start writing ourselves permission slips for things better left

alone. When I came to the Crossing, I followed a skillful leader
who had accomplished some groundbreaking things. However,
without humility he found himself caught up in compromises
of integrity that eventually led him into sexual misconduct.
The first thing that I did after coming to Quincy was rearrange
the offices so that anyone coming to see me had to pass by my
assistant. I had windows put in all office doors and established
a morality policy that any future employees would have to sign
off on. Compromises to integrity put all of the most valuable
things in our lives at risk. Paul warns the Ephesians saying,
*"But among you there must not even be hint of sexual immorality,
or of any kind of impurity, or of greed, because these are improper
for God's holy people." Ephesians 5:3* A high level of integrity
places a proper foundation for the skills a leader will need in
a micropolitan church.

There are already plenty of great books probably filling
your shelf about this subject. These ideas are nothing new.
Just see them in the light of a different setting. There are
a series of questions I need to ask. How you answer will
determine whether or not you have the basic building blocks
of a micropolitan church.

The first question is:

Is there a leader?

Churches in micropolitan communities struggle to have
leaders...or maybe I should say "true leaders". There is no
shortage of people who wear the badge. We have pastors,
elders, deacons, trustees, superintendents, and committee
chairman. Are you ready for a moment of truth? Just how
many of those spots are occupied by "true leaders"? So what
is a "true leader"?

I love leadership definitions. I once heard a great quote from an army general who said, "Leadership is taking people to a place they would have never have gone to by themselves." There's the problem! Without a true leader, these churches aren't going anywhere. The people wearing the badge are dug in and defending their ground. Another author wrote a statement defining a true leader saying, "Leaders lead!". Most churches in micropolitan communities are stalled because they have plenty of people called leaders filling roles established years ago for the right reason but remaining for one purpose: To maintain what already exists. Someone's definition of insanity is doing the same thing and expecting a different result. Churches in micropolitan communities that resist change are staring down the barrel of their own mortality. While resistance to change is something any church can identify with, it is more pronounced in a micropolitan community. There is just more inertia or felt resistance to change than in urban or metropolitan areas. Micropolitan communities that resist change become more irrelevant as businesses, jobs, and populations move out, creating decline. The church that doesn't embrace change stands to suffer the same fate as the community it serves. The changes so desperately needed require a "true leader" to help the church bring them to pass.

Without a leader casting a vision, a church can find itself in turbulent waters. We've all heard the King James version of Proverbs 29:18 quoted in discussions of vision, "Where there is no vision, the people perish." The NIV translation says, "Where there is no revelation, the people cast off restraint." Consider the word restraint. We usually see it as a negative word, but its use here suggests that when we forget *why* we're doing something, it no longer restrains us. Restraint is a good thing when it holds us to what we've pledged to do. We are restrained by our Master to fulfill His Great Commandment and Great Commission. Paul embraced this concept of restraint by calling himself a "*doulos*". It means a slave for life and a slave by choice. When our model becomes ineffective, we must remember that we are restrained to His mission. With so many years without change in the history books, we can become restrained to the wrong things and forget the whole reason we exist. Tradition has replaced the mission in many churches in micropolitan communities. A visionary leader is critical to call attention to the changes so desperately needed to keep the mission primary. The book of Judges gives us a sobering commentary on what happens without an effective leader for the people of God. The book ends with this passage, "In those days Israel had no king; everyone did as he saw fit."

Even with a true leader, a church in a micropolitan community is still looking at turbulent waters. Visionary leaders face an uphill battle even in healthy environments. Leadership that moves the church to change is seldom comfortable. It will mean moving away from the place where you are. This is almost never easy. Policies and structures will be adjusted or abandoned. Key positions will be established. Others will be replaced or removed. Change is best served in healthy times, but the institutional inertia and the success of years gone by prompt existing leaders to consider that if it isn't broken, why fix it? By the time many churches find the stomach to change, they are pretty far gone. Like a terminal cancer patient, they are willing to grasp for life with experimental treatments. In his great little book, *How The Mighty Fall*, Jim Collins discusses the downward spiral that leads once successful businesses to capitulation and death. His research shows that in an effort to reverse the fall, companies make sweeping changes. However, by the time they do it, they are over leveraged in the opposite direction and not healthy enough to manage the massive changes.

Any change is best accomplished in smaller increments. Driving even on a straight road requires constant corrections at the wheel. It may seem that you're going straight, but careful examination reveals a long line of small corrections.

Jerry Harris

By contrast, most of us have been distracted while driving only to be frantically forced into a major correction and a very dangerous situation. Big change divided up into lots of smaller, more manageable adjustments is a healthy strategy for churches. A Harvard professor defined leadership this way; "Leadership is making people uncomfortable at a rate that they can tolerate." What does this mean for a "true leader"? If you are already in a church in a micropolitan community that wants to change, do you have the patience for it? If you are thinking about going to one and implementing change, consider what already exists. Sometimes pastors have the same logic that a spouse does in a bad marriage. They think, "After we're married, I'll get him or her to change that behavior." That's a bad thing to bet your marriage or your career on. When interviewing with a church in a micropolitan community, find out what is on and off the table. Make an assessment of what is needed before you say "yes" and have a frank discussion about specifics with existing leaders. "Can we get rid of the pews, the pulpit, the choir loft, the choir, the choir director, the organ, the organist, the order of worship, the communion table?...What about the by-laws? Existing leaders will talk a great game about their desire for growth, but when specific changes are discussed, you'll get more honest answers. These are the reasons that the Crossing likes to establish new churches in micropolitans. Like an empty canvas, the absence of established traditions grants a freedom to explore edgy styles and methods.

The second question is:

Is there a vision?

I once heard Bill Hybels relate a story about a church member looking for advice in struggling with his pastor. His frustration was born out of his pastor's lack of vision. Exasperated, he declared, "Just put a target on the wall...any

40

target on any wall!" People need to experience purpose in their relationship with Christ and effective leaders must set goals reflecting their vision for the church creating that purpose. I'm not saying that vision is as simple as filling in the blank. Vision isn't an afterthought. A leader's vision for the church is the most important tool he possesses in living out his call to ministry. A vision is something you get married to. It's going to define you. It finishes statements like, "We are the church that......" *Vision is not building a building, a new worship style, or a new marketing strategy. Vision is revelatory! It's a God-given conviction that gives purpose to the position of leadership.*

The first time I went through the "Experiencing God" workbook and class, I had been in ministry for 15 years. I thought I was "doing it right". If someone would have asked me what my vision was, I think I could have come up with a good answer. I don't think that outside of simple obedience, any particular vision was driving me. But as I plowed through that workbook something very personal and powerful occurred. I began to realize that Christians were going through their whole life never understanding that they could have an intimate, personal relationship with Jesus Christ. The words stuck inside heart: ...intimate...personal...relationship...with Jesus Christ. I saw Christian people committed to going through the motions, professional at putting up the front, but missing out on deep change. That study began forming a vision for me to break down every barrier standing between every person and that intimate, personal relationship with Jesus. I knew that couldn't happen doing business as usual. It required change. I cast the vision before elders of the church. I remember saying, "We have to do whatever it takes to help people to find an intimate personal relationship with Jesus Christ." Just the idea of the kind of potential changes that would need to take place in the church to remove those barriers was enough to give the elders pause. After a while, I realized that the necessary changes that needed to happen to make the vision a reality weren't going to happen at that church. With this vision inside me, I wasn't going to be able to honor God doing business as usual. If a vision is revelatory, nothing will stop it. For me, it meant moving out of an 11-year ministry to a new location to give it a chance to happen. There are a lot of great things that have happened at the Crossing and every one of them has been driven by that vision. *All I want is to help people discover an intimate, personal relationship with Jesus Christ. Micropolitan wasn't and isn't the vision. Mega-church isn't. Multi-site isn't. Missional isn't. They are all just a means or method of achieving the vision God gave me. They are connected to the vision because they give form and function to it. They are the mechanisms that make the vision a reality. A vision is what sums us up.*

The third question is:

Are you passionate about your vision?

If you aren't passionate about your vision, you don't have a vision. Passion is what validates your investment into your vision. Passion is why God inspired John to put the word "so" in front of "loved" in John 3:16. Passion is what caused the Father to see the prodigal son while he was still a long way off and run to His son. Passion is what holds your commitment to something when logic and reason fail you. Passion is preoccupying. Your mind is running constantly back to it. It takes an effort to think about something else. Passion is personal. It attaches itself to your own identity and it becomes self-defining. Passion is emotional; it's hard to talk about it without inflection in your voice or getting caught in hyperbole. Passion is powerful. Like a ship going through the water, it creates a wake that people get caught up in. When a vision is doused with passion, you're getting pretty close to all you need for a roaring fire.

A church service should be filled with passion. I've often said, "How can someone be in the presence of God and stay the same?" And yet, there are plenty of people that don't change at all. Maybe there is unresolved sin, divided attention, or a closed-off heart blocking His presence. But maybe it's the fault of those of us who call ourselves leaders. Maybe we've lost our passion.

Ephesus was a passionate church in the midst of a passionate people. The picture of the church's elders weeping over Paul in Acts 20 is riveting. If you could choose a New Testament church to be a member of, it would be hard to beat Ephesus. They were doing it right. It's revealed so brilliantly in Paul's letter to them. Paul stayed there 2 years...longer there as a pastor than anywhere else. Later, John used Ephesus as a base of operations for managing all the churches of Asia Minor. Jesus' mother actually lived there. The church became a critical metropolitan hub for infant Christianity. The church is approaching 50 years old at the end of the 1st century. She still looks great from the outside as she obediently goes through the motions but something essential is missing. According to Revelation 2:4-6 she's lost her first love...her passion. Jesus is making it clear that there really was no point in existing without it. What a perfect picture of so many churches in micropolitan communities. Still healthy, somewhat effective, and obedient to a fault, many churches in micropolitans have lost the passionate vision they once had. Vision has been replaced by tradition, and passion by obedient maintenance. To illustrate this point, I planned a sermon to be interrupted by dimming lights, soft music, a disco ball, and a couple in tux and formal dancing to *The Very Thought of You*. I acted as if I'd been interrupted and told them to sit down. Lost in each other's eyes, they completely ignored me. As I complained, a church member yelled at me to sit down! When the song was over, they strolled away holding hands and continuing their gaze. I returned to the sermon saying that the love that Jesus wants is captivating, preoccupying, and passionate. Passion rekindles the flame in our hearts for Jesus and His mission. Like the Ephesian church, our vision is pointless without passion.

Jerry Harris

The fourth question is:

Can you communicate your vision?

When we were first dreaming of going to Macomb, IL with The Crossing, I took our pastoral staff up to survey possible locations. We were eating at a Mexican restaurant close by. The lunch crowd was filling up the place with businessmen, students taking a break from campus food, families eating together, and so on. While we waited on our order I told them to look around and imagine how many of those people were members of our church and just didn't know it yet. How many marriages and families were going to be saved, how many victories over addictions, and how many students forever changed were in that room? There was something epic and dramatic about seeing it that way. It was like seeing it with God's eyes. When leaders are passionately preoccupied with their vision, they are always looking for opportunities to communicate it.

Effective communication of vision happens when ownership transfers to those receiving it. There is dialogue in the conversation. The effective communicator tries to help the receiver make the vision his or her own. He will frame the vision in contexts familiar to the receiver. I see this illustrated dramatically in the preaching event. *I believe the best sermons that people hear are the ones they don't hear.* Confused? Let me explain. We all believe the Holy Spirit is working in the Word of God as it is delivered, but I see something more. I'm preaching and the congregation is listening. Each one is listening with their own set of circumstances, challenges, and emotions. Something trips in the listener's mind. Maybe it's a word, a phrase, or a thought that comes from what they are hearing. Suddenly, they are attaching that thought to their own personal experience. They aren't listening to me anymore. The Holy Spirit has taken over the controls. This is the richest moment because something new is attaching itself to the soul of the listener. The experience runs its course and the listener finds the on-ramp back into the sermon. Before long, another trigger starts the next rich moment. People have come up to me after sermons sharing a point that affected them deeply only to find me staring back at them realizing I never said what they heard. What's happening? They are making the sermon theirs. It may not look the same as when you gave it. That's not really important. What is important is what happened between them and God. That's intimate, personal, and relational with Jesus.

The same thing is needed when communicating vision. The listener gets caught up in the power and passion of the vision. The most effective ideas communicated are the ones that people consider their own. The best leaders have learned to be comfortable with adjustments to means and methods or with entirely new ones. Remember, the vision hasn't changed, just the way to carry it out. Very few things look like I imagined them at our church. They look a lot better. While I'm willing to die on the hill for the vision, I get excited about how leaders around me adjust the means and methods making it their own. If the leader has this all figured out beforehand, he fails to capitalize on a great opportunity of developing the leaders around him. Everybody owns the vision through the means and methods they've developed to achieve it. Everyone shares in the success produced. Everyone realizes that only Jesus works through the body of Christ like this.

When a vision is communicated effectively, people are drawn to the vision and not just the leader. In the long term, this gets far more traction for the church and for the kingdom of God. I know this sounds like a contradiction because a passionate vision is personal, but a great leader gets people to focus on the vision itself. Churches that center on a vision are going to be much healthier than those that center on the personality of a leader. Letting the focus rest on the leader is ultimately and invariably destructive. Leaders are humans and humans can't help but make mistakes, be inconsistent, and disappoint. Concentrating on the vision puts the focus on God where it belongs. He alone is consistently faithful and true.

I want to mention one last thing about leaders in micropolitan churches. The normal look of leadership in a local church is a group of staff and a group of lay leaders. There will probably be some form of regular staff meetings and regular lay leadership meetings (board meetings). Both of these circles of leadership are critically important. The "true leader" leads through these groups. He has the responsibility of keeping these two circles connected by building great relationships inside of both. He not only facilitates each one in the circles to reach a higher potential, but also promotes mutual respect between groups as they own each achievement together.

Think Outward

An outward focus is absolutely critical to the micropolitan church. To focus outward means that the church's primary concern is the people outside it's walls and influence. It means that the church's assets; it's money, it's talent, it's time; and it's facility is used up reaching into that group. Every church will tell you that they have an outward focus. They know that Jesus' great commandment and great commission is clear about it. The painful reality is that even though churches would claim to be outward, their activity, teaching, finances, ministries, and even architecture tell a different story. There is a gravity that pulls the church inward where the concerns are for those inside its walls. Church budgets reflect most of the money spent to minister to the saved. The building is filled with classrooms used only an hour or two a week. The songs chosen for worship are the ones church people know and love. Church boards and by-laws are designed to keep it that way, being weighed down with bureaucracy and tradition. Any changes to reach out in new ways are quickly squelched by the status quo. The fact that very few unfamiliar faces appear in church is a constant reminder of missing the mark. Many of these traditional churches are so afraid of how change would affect the usual that they would rather curse the darkness than venture out into the darkness and light a candle. I know that I'm being hard on the inwardly focused church, but after spending 11 years pastoring one, I think I understand why they are the way they are.

Virtually everything else in society is in a constant state of motion, reinventing itself again and again. As I previously wrote, people live in micropolitans for a reason. Part of that reason is a slower pace. Of all the institutions in a community, the church represents one of the most stable. Its stability is tied to its resistance to change. Many view that stability like the feel of an old pair of jeans or a comfortable blanket to wrap up in. It's safe and predictable, like an oasis in a crazy world surrounding you with happy memories and generations old friendships. It's a lot to give up for people who don't value what you do. Even so, Jesus didn't call His children to personal comfort but to His commandment and commission.

Some might see this approach as out of balance. Don't we have a responsibility to those who have come into a relationship with Christ to take care of them? My experience has taught me that when we concern ourselves with the needs that God has called us to, He will take care of ours. When we focus on our own needs, we not only marginalize our God-given responsibility, we replace dependence on Him for independence. We push Him out of all the ways we experience Him meeting our needs. The children of Israel were punished to wander in the desert for 40 years because of the fear that replaced their faith in God. For me, Numbers 14:3 records what pushed God over the line. It says, *"If only we had died in Egypt! Or in this desert! Why is the Lord bringing us to this land only let us fall by the sword? Our wives and our children will be taken as plunder."* Their lack of faith was in God's ability to take care of them, especially the weakest of them. God responded by granting their request. Every one of them with the exception of two spies died in that desert and the children (that God was considered incapable of providing for) were the ones who took the land 40 years later. When we cast all our cares on Him, expending our energy being outwardly focused, I would have a hard time believing that God wouldn't honor that in a mighty way.

For an outwardly focused church, the competition is not the other churches in the area. The competition is every other available use of time. For people outside of an intimate, personal relationship with Jesus Christ, Sunday is a great day to sleep in, read a good book, or just spend time with family. It's an opportunity to get some of those chores crossed off the list or get over last night's hangover. An outwardly focused church confronts the question, "Why would I give up these other things to come to church?". Is there something more valuable there that would justify me spending some of most important currency I have...my time?

Most people have already answered that question. The answer is based upon a pre-conceived notion of what church is. Honestly, the church is fighting an uphill battle in American culture. In his book *Unchristian*, David Kinnaman explores the views a younger subset (16-25years old) of culture as it measures the church. In short, his research shows an un-churched population that sees the church as hypocritical, not really living out its own rules and ideals. They see it having an agenda to "get people saved" without a genuine concern for real or long-lasting relationships with them. The church is seen as homophobic, sheltered, too political, and judgmental.7 Even though we would argue with these perceptions, there is no denying that many churches are either shrinking or closing, failing to figure out ways to bridge the cultural gap and remain uncompromising with Biblical truth. Prognosticators present a pretty dismal future the church.

Churches have a hard time engaging the prevailing culture. It's not an easy road and certainly not business as usual. First, it's hard to hit a moving target. Culture is constantly morphing requiring never-ending adjustments and evaluation. It requires exploration of changes that reach down into things maybe not doctrinal but nevertheless understood as foundational. Instead of embracing the changes necessary to engage the culture we find ourselves in, we end up competing with each other for those who already attend church. We try to build a better mousetrap so to speak. That's why the majority of growth in American churches is no growth at all…even in megachurches. It is simply people moving from one church to another. The Quincy community has about 20% of its people in one of its 85 churches on a given weekend. The religious establishment is German Catholic and Lutheran. While these churches aren't growing, their roots go down deep. There are 8 Catholic parishes in town as well as a Catholic University, a Catholic High School, Western Catholic Charities, and the largest church in the diocese. There are Christian radio and television stations. *The outwardly focused church doesn't compete with churches or the religious culture but instead redefines the mission to the 80% who don't care to go anywhere.* It markets itself in non-Christian places. It builds bridges with the community to earn the opportunity to make a first impression. It doesn't take that first impression for granted.

While these realities hold true for any church, it is a place where a micropolitan church can really find an advantage. Change is a hard and potentially a very dangerous thing, but those who can master changes for outward focus will be in the sweet spot of a micropolitan community. Traditional churches resist change and chances are that there hasn't been a church in the community to break out of the mold. A micropolitan church stands a good chance of holding a monopoly on a new and fresh approach.

The Crossing found a monopoly in this effort. After over 11 years and with 2400 people attending just at the Quincy campus, no other church in the area has even made the attempt. Whether it was having services in well-known community venues and leaving a perfectly good facility behind just to find some common ground with people, or producing TV spots and buying key time to show it, the goal was to draw in that 80%. We held Easter services in Quincy's largest venue to get an opportunity to make that first impression on neutral ground. Reading books like *The Purpose Driven Church* provided our leadership with an adaptable template for change that fit us. We moved in the direction of attractive, market-based mega-churches. We visited them; setting up meetings with our counterparts to benchmark ideas we thought would work. Using these tools, we set up an evolving model for our weekend experiences.

Getting into the Shoes of the 80%

One of the key components that the Crossing learned from the megachurches we visited was to create an environment where the 80% felt free to let their defenses down. The church and especially its leaders have to make a daily commitment to get in the shoes of the 80%. We can't lose touch of how the world looks and feels in their shoes. If you are a Christian, you may have never had an Islamic experience. How would you feel driving into an Islamic Center's parking lot? What would it be like walking through the door? How would you be viewed? Where should you go? How should you conduct yourself? These are the some of the same questions going through the minds of the 80%. No doubt the defenses would be up. We wanted to create an environment where they would come down. The 80% also have a set of presuppositions of what a church looks and feels like. We took away the "churchy" feel by removing hymnals, pews, stained glass, pulpit, choir loft, etc. We put in comfortable chairs, controllable lighting, a good sound system and turned up the volume, used a computer and video for worship, and put the suits and dresses away. Without a pulpit and dressing down, we broke through hypocritical preacher stereotypes. Turning down the lights gave the 80% anonymity. Raising the volume allowed them to experiment with singing without others hearing them. We extended the invitation time and gave people the opportunity to come forward and do business with God without anyone bothering them. Although this was a confrontational moment, it became profound as people put movement together with life change. Defenses came down and Jesus came in. In the process, a new dynamic emerged.

The 80% Invite the 80%

That part of the 80% we were able to connect with liked church well enough to risk inviting their friends. I think we forget that those of us who have been Christians a while have probably already invited most of the people we know. Once your church breaks through into the 80%, big things are going to start to happen. Very quickly, I was hearing compliments like, "Helluva sermon today, Jerry!" or "You really kicked a** today!" Discovering what you have attracted is a moment of truth for the church. It tests the resolve of your commitment to the great commandment and commission. Programs started reflecting the needs of the 80%. The needs were many and varied. The unchurched and new Christians come with lots of baggage. They aren't givers. Our tracking shows that giving lags at least 18 months behind attendance. Committed Christians have to dig deeper, put up with approaches that don't fit them, and lose their comfort zone…and for what?…to watch a person change right before you eyes as Jesus touches him! Wow!! That's my bigger yes! I will give up what is comfortable and usual for that. If a leader can keep that vision, that "bigger yes" in front of the church and they are buying what he's selling, God will move!

You're feeling the natural resistance. The gravity is pulling you back but your heart is feeling the calling. There is a tension forming as those two forces pull all the slack out of your life and ministry. I know what you're inclined to say. You've heard all this before. It's the inch deep, mile wide church…a church full of consumers instead of disciples. But when you think about it, that's how we all start out, physically and spiritually. All a baby knows is what it needs. "Feed me, change me, burp me, hold me, love me." Why should it be any different spiritually? It's only a tragedy if it stays that way. If we have a plan to attract but no method to disciple, we miss the whole point. Jesus didn't call us to win converts, but to make disciples. We'll discuss that later. Interestingly, traditional churches are guilty of the very thing that they accuse outwardly focused churches of. They are full of consumers …they are just consuming a different product that is unappealing to the 80%. Traditional churches hold on to their traditions because it's what they like! How is that not self-serving and consumerist? The difference is that they disguise tradition for truth, stand on it like a soapbox, and justify virtually the same behavior.

While plenty of options exist in metropolitan or suburban church environments to find the "just right" church feel, micropolitans are not nearly as option-filled. There is an incredible field of spiritual harvest all around us if we have the courage to recognize and respond to it. The micropolitan community is especially fertile and fruitful because of the absence of those options and the pre-conceived notions of the 80%. Eleven years ago we started down this path and have yet to see any church in our community even attempt to duplicate it. Thousands of people later, there is no indication that we have gotten anywhere close to the end of its potential.

Think Downward

The church has a daunting task in its effort to minister to anyone who walks through the doors. The concept of targeting any particular age group or need at the expense of another isn't very palatable for most. No one wants anyone to be left out or marginalized. We rest in Paul's words from I Corinthians 9 "becoming all things to all men…", but however thoughtful and compassionate, that scripture is misapplied. It's really all about outward focus as seen at the end of each phrase. Paul becomes all things to win as many as possible. When a church looks at approach, it quickly hits the dilemma of how to effectively minister to the needs of its people across the board and the truth is, it's going to do some things better than others. Church boardrooms are filled with arguments about who to be relevant to ranging from how the money is spent, the type of music being played, the style of the sermon, to the clothes the preacher wears. If our goal is to please the people that are already there, choices are going to be made in all of these areas defining a target. This is the basis of most of the business of the inwardly focused church.

Most people in their 60's and 70's have been broken to a completely different approach that what we see in most attractional churches. As a matter of fact, every generation finds a different style or approach comfortable. Outward churches have taken the focus off what people on the inside want, focusing instead on the needs of the 80% on the outside. There is an equally important dimension to outward focus. I call this philosophy of downward focus "the dot".

The Dot

Whether we mean to or we do it by accident, every church puts out a product that is more effective to at least some subset of people. Every church has a target. It may not be intentional, as traditions tend to take on a life of their own but it's there just the same. Look at the style of your music and worship. Who is attracted to it? Look at the church budget. Who gets the most money? Look at the use of the building. Who gets the most space? Look at the style of the building and it's furniture. Is it antique? Does it have colors popular in the 1970's? Your church will tell you whom you are targeting. Now look at who is sitting in the seats. Don't figure in children under 12, as they have to go wherever their parents drive them. What is their average age? Don't speculate! Do your homework and give an honest answer. When you put all that together, you will know whom you are targeting. You may not like the answer but you need to face it. That is your dot. Now find an age range of about 5 years with 2 and 1/2 years on either side of the dot. Is it averaging the early 30's or the late 60's? You can get a hard number for this. Have you got it? Great! Now, if you want to do ministry the same way you have been, you'll continue to be effective with that age group of people. How close are they to dying? Let's say 80. If your dot is 55, it means that your church has 25 years to live. It's mortal. If the church continues doing the same thing, in 25 years it will only be relevant to the people in the cemetery. That's a sobering thought but nonetheless very important to understand. Many churches in micropolitan communities wonder why they are getting older and smaller. This is the reason.

Unless you have figured out how to make the sun stand still, time will continue to march on relentlessly. As time marches on, the dot will move with it. The dot is bound to time as long as we continue to be most relevant to the same people. The only way to change this is to change the target.

If the church can focus the target downward, time won't slow down but the dot will. Our goal is to stop the dot from moving at all. I know a church that was doing things today as they did in 1980. In those days they were on the cutting edge. They sang their hymns faster than anyone, used overheads for the words, had a moveable pulpit, and used chairs instead of pews. It worked so well! The building was filled with young families in their late 20's and early 30's. It worked so well, they stuck with it. They are still doing the same thing in virtually the same way. The only difference is that those who were once in their early 30's are turning 60! They love it but no one is accusing them of being on the cutting edge anymore. Young families are thin...but there's plenty of money. The more time they allow between what they are doing and the change that is necessary, the target gets farther away and the corrections become to big to manage. Guess where they will be in 2030 if something doesn't change?

How do we get the dot to stop moving? You can't stop time...but you can stop the dot. The way to do it is by focusing downward. We must continually look to be the most relevant to the people who are approaching where your dot presently is, not the ones already there. It keeps you stretching downward to adjust to new ways to be relevant. This forces the church to look at the changing culture and adapt to it. There is no need to compromise doctrine or vision, just the means and methods of how they are delivered. It means we have to embrace new forms of technology, new styles of music and worship, hire younger staff members, spend more money and expend more energy in programming in that direction. When outward and downward focuses are coupled together, the church has set itself up for immortality. If the dot isn't moving, even though there are people in the church getting older, the church isn't getting older. Coupled with an outward focus, there is a steady stream of the 80% coming into a relationship with Christ being attracted by the relevance defined by the dot.

The obvious question is, aren't we neglecting the people on the other side of the dot? What about their needs? How can that be right? Look a little closer at the dynamic. As people approach the age range where the dot is, everything is becoming more and more relevant. You are getting the maximum impact for your work. As things begin making more and more sense for the person, they are getting into the dot. This is the place when our hearts are the most open, we're the most teachable, and discipleship traits like worship, ministry, prayer, and Bible study really revs up. Those 5 or so years are absolutely critical to discipleship. While we're there, the church has to establish proper priorities, values, and a Christian world- view in the hearts of targeted people. In the dot, people learn how important people without an intimate, personal relationship with Jesus really are to Him. They develop disciplines to value spiritual change in others more than personal comfort. They get involved by committing to be part of the solution by discovering their shape in ministry and putting it into practice. It's a critical time because before long, we're moving out of it. We can't stop the march of time in our own lives. The goal is that by the time the church is becoming less personally relevant to us, we have traded in our own needs for the "bigger yes" of seeing the effectiveness of the church and our own ministry on those coming up. We incorporate our gifts into the rest of the body as we join together to reach into the lives of those hearts coming into full bloom. The question at the beginning of this paragraph asked about people on the upward side of the dot. If the church has done its job, there really isn't a problem. *It's not about us anymore. That is a simple definition of Christian maturity.* Guess what else is happening? The church is becoming immortal because while time marches on, the dot is either moving downward or holding steady.

I can't overemphasize just how important it is to communicate this philosophy to the leaders and congregation. It goes beyond what we're doing to answer the question of why.

When we know "why" it gives substance to our purpose. We're making a difference that's going to outlive us. When we look hard at it, we know better than to be self-centered. Now we're not looking at a church an inch deep and a mile wide. Look at how much change Jesus endured to become human.

Let us fix our eyes on Jesus, the Author and Perfecter of our faith, Who for the joy set before Him endured the cross, scorning its shame, and sat down at the right hand of the throne of God. Consider Him Who endured such opposition from sinful men, so that you sill not grow weary and lose heart. Hebrews 12: 2-3

The joy set before Him was sharing eternity with us. Let's find our joy is sharing eternity with His lost children.

Focusing outward and downward is what makes the church attractional. These attributes are magnified in a micropolitan community because they more than likely will exist in a religious vacuum. Its countercultural dynamic makes it magnetic. Other churches won't follow suit because the investment is too great or the change too severe. Micropolitan communities have a major appetite for this because of the lack of alternatives. The 80% will become your exclusive territory. Some will find the changes uncomfortable. They will want to look to what is more comfortable for them. That's okay! You will always lose people with change, but you will also exponentially gain. Losing people is rarely a positive experience, but losing them for this strategy is a worthy trade. Losing the saved to win the lost isn't a bad deal because whether they attend your church or not, the saved are still saved. Those in opposition to this kind of aggressive strategy will find plenty of other comfortable places to worship. It is important that you communicate that there are plenty of other churches in the community where one can worship, but that we feel called to this "bigger yes" of the 80%. Sometimes the worst thing that can happen is for frustrated people to stay. Micropolitan churches are gracious in showing the door to those more internally focused. The Crossing has been a real help in growing churches around us with transfers of Christians uncomfortable with this strategy and it certainly hasn't slowed us down.

Jerry Harris

Think Relevant

As I discussed earlier, every church is relevant, so to speak. There is a target that every church is reaching, whether accidentally or on purpose. The real question is who are they relevant to? An understanding of who the target presently is will go a long way in determining growth, influence, and the general effectiveness level of the church in it's environment. For instance, if a church is targeting people over the age of 65, they will be thinking about using technology to make services accessible for the hearing impaired more than replacing the hymnals. They will change the length of the service in consideration of how long an attender could manage sitting in the pew rather than evaluating attention span. They might resist small groups in favor of Sunday school classes as empty nesters have downsized their home and are more used to peace and quiet.

If a church is targeting 18-25 year olds, choices will again reflect a relevant approach. Smaller more relational environments like a café conducive to meeting new people, self-expression, or establishing intimate relationships fits perfectly. This target will have high expectations of excellence but will not be able to generate the money to achieve them so smaller or rented facilities work best. Many will struggle in ministry commitment as they maintain their mobility, still searching for that perfect fit in career path. Programming will need to be simple and transferable to fit into that mobility. Ministries to children, teens, or families would be a low priority.

So the challenge for the church that wants to have maximum effectiveness in a micropolitan community is to find the sweet spot of that community. Jorge is a student pastor at Christ Fellowship in Miami, Florida. The population in that metropolitan community is primarily Hispanic. I was listening as some of our student pastors were sharing with him at dinner. Jorge related that student ministry in a Hispanic community requires a far different approach than in a primarily white community. Hispanic families in his community are very close knit, sharing most experiences together. When Jorge plans a student event, he has to plan on parents attending and participating. In the Midwest, Student pastors and students zealously protect the distance between them and their parents in most programming. When the target changes, the definition of relevance and the approach that follows must change.

Since most churches in micropolitan communities are holding on to their individual or denominational traditions, people who wish to attend them are required to adjust their expectations accordingly. The majority of the community, the 80%, doesn't care about those traditions and will just write them off as out of touch. That is beginning of finding the sweet spot of relevance for a micropolitan church. Questions must be asked to find a profile for that 80%. If the desire is to bring as many of this 80% into an intimate, personal relationship with Christ, they will determine what is relevant.

Many Christians have become "institutionalized". It isn't that we don't want to be relevant to people outside the church, we've just been out of that world so long, we just don't remember it. Many churches in micropolitan communities are only growing through the children their young families are having. While being born in the church has some great advantages, one disadvantage is a lack of understanding of the world of the 80%. When we were in the planning stages of launching in Macomb, IL, we considering partnering with a local campus ministry. I had the opportunity to meet with several of their board members to cast the vision for our church and what we might do cooperatively. I was particularly excited because the campus ministry was almost completely made up of students coming out of area churches and wanting a spiritually safe environment on a secular campus. One of the board members was vocally resistant. He said that the campus ministry was by students and for students and that having students ministering to people outside that target wasn't something he was in favor of. I asked him what he felt like he was accomplishing for the kingdom of God. He said that they were training up lay leaders for the church. I remember thinking to myself that these would be exactly the worst leaders for tomorrow's church. Their ministry focus was primarily self-serving, completely disregarding the much more than 80% on that university campus that had no relationship with Jesus.

The Crossing found our sweet spot of relevance more pragmatically than philosophically. We found it in the success of the megachurch. Say what you want about the depth of the megachurch, the fact that they know how to attract people is not disputable. Since attraction and introduction are the first steps in an intimate, personal relationship with Jesus, I considered them the experts on the subject. They had struck a relevant chord in a very large percentage of those 80%. Instead of holding an unreasonable expectation that the 80% would suddenly and miraculously find the church doing things the way they had always done it interesting, megachurches looked across the board at finding relevant means and methods to package timeless truth.

We chose to look at megachurches because they had simply found ways to get people in the door. They are relevant to today's culture. The American megachurch is almost exclusively an urban and suburban phenomenon. Although these churches are greatly varied in church affiliation and denominational roots, their approach is quite similar. They are defined as having a regular attendance of over 2000 a weekend.

The front door is wide open in the megachurch and people are walking through it in droves.

The Hartford Institute study says that the megachurch movement shows no signs of slowing. Almost 90% of megachurches are growing, and many at exponential rates.[8] The question is, "How do they do it?" There have been plenty of books and models shared over the past few years that seek to answer that question. Churches that followed approaches developed by pioneers like Bill Hybels and Rick Warren found their churches growing. Books like "Inside the Mind of Unchurched Harry and Mary" and "The Purpose-Driven Church" became staples of a megachurch approach. Over the years, cultural prognosticators and religious commentators of post-modernism have forecasted the demise of the megachurch, but number crunching of the hard data shows that the megachurch movement indicates no signs of slowing. We were looking for a way do them in a micropolitan way. There weren't any books about that. Here are some of the attributes we saw:

Megachurches are Attractive.

Virtually every part of the church has a marketing flavor about it. Parking lots are well marked and filled with volunteer attendants eager to help. Lobbies are inviting with the smell of designer coffee. Well thought out conversation areas, information kiosks, and sign-up stations line the walls. Carefully placed posters describe the next big event. Bathrooms are easy to find with plenty of room and spotlessly clean. The children's areas are theme based and have an amusement park look with discovery zone style play areas in bright colors. There are security systems in place to ensure the welfare of the children. Check-in stations are computerized. Auditoriums have a theater feel with comfortable seats. The technology is cutting edge with intelligent lighting, smoke machines, and multiple video screens. The music is contemporary and highly professional. Images are magnified on the screen with easy to read words to the worship songs. Some have amenities like workout rooms, art and dance classes, bookstores and snack shops. There are plenty of ways to get connected. You can join a motorcycle club, moms in touch, divorce recovery, or a girl's night out. Opportunities abound to make a difference in the community with literally hundreds of ministries to fit every passion. All of this and so much more is available and all they do is take a free-will offering. Is there a better deal out there?

Megachurches are Inclusive.

Not only do megachurches present an attractive atmosphere, they work hard to break down barriers that many traditional churches have grown comfortable with. Most megachurches have a "come as you are" mentality. The fact that there is no dress code is modeled by staff and volunteers. They are not proponents of rules and regulations and lines between committed members and first-time attenders. They have done away with service components that would alienate newcomers. There are services at different times of the day or week to fit into crammed schedules. They resist spiritual jargon so as to level the playing field. Megachurches don't use terms like "the lost" or "unbelievers" to define people without a relationship with Jesus. They don't argue about differences between Christian denominations. They are always looking for the common ground or a point of connection to build a bridge rather than to burn one. They connect sermons to cultural catch phrases or topics that are very practical in nature. Programming is targeted for people with specific needs.

Megachurches are Exciting.

Megachurches radiate a feeling of joy. Joy was the #1 attribute used to describe megachurch worship.**9** This was followed by a sense of God's presence, a thought-provoking atmosphere, and a welcoming environment. All these build an excitement that fuels a desire to attend. People are afraid they will "miss something" if they take a week off. The American megachurch is a great thing to share with friends. What emerges from taking the chance to invite a friend and then seeing their approval is very exciting. Megachurches give a missional view to their people about the world around them. The idea of making a real difference can be incredibly exciting to people compared the 40-hour grind of their workweek. It can be as close as a food pantry or as far as a third world short-term mission trip. Every week there is something new. The freshness draws a sharp contrast with the perceived staleness of a traditional church that can cause a migration of sorts.

Jerry Harris

***So how does a micropolitan church capitalize
on the success of megachurch and put their
ideas to work for the Kingdom of God?***

First of all, all these attributes in a metropolitan or suburban area are expected. Everything else in the culture is demanding excellence. You have nearly infinite choices in restaurants. Just think of all the kinds available. Growing up in Indianapolis, I remember the amazing selection. You could be locked up in a pseudo jail and have a great tenderloin. I remember a place called *Caves and Caverns* that had a prehistoric theme. A restaurant named *Illusions* came with a tableside magic show. There were great jazz clubs, comedy clubs, strip clubs, dance clubs....*The Spaghetti Factory*, and *Hard Rock Café*. There were restaurants known for their food specialty, their ethnicity, or their atmosphere. There were restaurants that had decades-old reputations and brand new ones. They cooked food on wood fire, flaming grills, or hibachi's with acrobatic knife-handlers.

This is not the case in Quincy, IL. Although there are some great places to eat, there is really no comparison. The point is that people expect that kind of selection in Indianapolis but resign themselves to what is there in rural America.

Churches in metropolitan communities are similar to their restaurants...something for everybody. When a church in a micropolitan community begins acting like a megachurch, it is unexpected and exciting. In towns where there aren't very many "latest things", churches like the Crossing will always stand out. Rethinking the church in the micropolitan community and adapting the proven methods of the megachurch to fit has proven to be even more powerful than in a metropolitan setting. The two main reasons for this are institutional inertia and the lack of competition. These are exclusive to a micropolitan. There is no need to reinvent the wheel...it just needs to be adapted to a smaller setting, staff, and budget.

All of this is easy to say but a lot harder to actually do. But take heart. Another beautiful thing about a micropolitan church embracing these ideas is that the community rarely has anything close to compare it to. There is a lot of grace in that. If you're using volunteers to run programs and equipment that most megachurches have paid staff for, there are going to be plenty of mistakes. No problem! There's nothing to compare it to locally.

I once heard John Maxwell make a statement that has always resonated with me. He said, "Anything worth doing is worth doing poorly." He illustrated the statement using Michael Jordan being cut from the Jr. High basketball team. The Jr. High is probably named after him now. We never start at the top of our game. It has to come to us as we adapt, overcome, and evolve. A micropolitan community will give you the room that a metropolitan won't. Metropolitan people can just go down the street.

Now don't get me wrong. The main reason that the megachurch model appeals to me is their power of attraction. I don't see much more value as far as attraction beyond that, but that in itself is a great thing! The way that an attractional church grows is by keeping the front door open wider than the back door. The difference between those two numbers is the rate of growth. That is why the megachurch is primarily a metropolitan occurrence. Since the population is so large, there is always a source for plenty more in the front door. I have a problem with this for this reason. Growth is not the point! Making disciples is what Christianity is all about. Attractional churches are bringing in consumers, nothing more. It's what happens after they are brought in that is important and lasting. When Jesus worked miracles of healing or feeding the hungry huge crowds were attracted, but when they were called to commitment, they left. Jesus got more done to change the world out of 12 committed guys than he ever did from those huge crowds! Recently, Buffalo Wild Wings came to Quincy. For the first month I didn't even try to eat there. It was crammed with people inside and outside waiting to get a seat. My patience paid off. After a while, the newness of a new restaurant wore off and it was just another place to eat. If a micropolitan church puts all its effort into being attractional, eventually the newness will wear off and little will have been gained.

Greg Hawkins, in Willow Creek's "Reveal" has worked with many churches doing countless surveys to figure out why people go out the back door. He looks at "mature Christians" leaving and is trying to answer the question of why they don't stay. But just because someone has been going to church a long time, participated on committees, or involved themselves in ministry doesn't make them mature. Any rural pastor could tell you that. Maturity comes when "it's not about you anymore." *The worst kind of believer is the one who is convinced he's mature when he's just a consumer with a developed taste.* Micropolitan churches don't have the luxury of keeping the front door open wider than the back because the population well is far shallower. And besides that, it's just plain wrong. The only reason I can tolerate people going out the back door is because they have made a conscious decision to step away from our vision or doctrinal values.

I embrace attraction, but I have to remind myself that it has a shelf life. Something more substantial has to replace it or it will eventually wear off. Attractional approaches last longer in micropolitan communities than in metropolitan ones simply because of the lack of options, but unless we follow it up with a great discipleship approach that works, we may be doing more harm than good. Unless we define maturity properly, sophisticated consumers will misunderstand where they are, and when the church doesn't consider their continuing needs a priority, they will leave. A micropolitan church takes advantage of the relevance of megachurch models to attract the 80% but attaches it to intentional, relational discipleship. Attraction is only the beginning of a great adventure.

Think Discipleship

"What would happen if for whatever reason, you no longer had the use of your building? How would that affect your church?" That was a question that Jim Putman, senior pastor of Real Life Ministries in Post Falls, Idaho asked me recently. I was there investigating the incredible growth I'd heard about in that church under Jim's leadership. Real Life had grown from just a few families at it's birth in 1998 to just under 9000 ten years later. That in itself is amazing, but what takes it over the top is that Post Falls is a micropolitan community of about 40,000.

I had the opportunity to meet Jim in Denver at a leader retreat a few months before and was invited to come and check it out. He had also just released a book on Real Life's approach called *Church is a Team Sport* that I had freshly read. I had no idea what I was setting myself up for being unprepared for just how anti-attractional it was. We had to go through a small neighborhood to get to the parking lot. The building was a large, brick covered rectangle without any fancy architecture. It was attached to formerly outgrown older buildings and a couple of modular units. Moving into the lobby, instead of inviting kiosks, there was the familiar sight of simple folding tables and posters for sign-ups, an added-in bookstore, and round plywood topped banquet tables for people to meet around. The auditorium was a gymnasium with the stage in the corner, fold out aluminum bleachers on two sides, stage in the corner, and not much in the way of cutting edge technology. I was completely confused and a little irritated. There was little about this that was attractive.

Now back to the initial question. Jim said that if the building were gone tomorrow, their church would be just fine. I knew I couldn't say that. We had become building dependent, staff dependent, and technology dependent. Most of our structure depended on attracting new people using these three components. Jim had built Real Life in a different way. All the emphasis was placed on discipleship primarily happening in small groups. He even said that if there had to be a choice, he would prefer his people attending their small group instead of weekend worship. All of this was hitting me sideways.

Since I've always considered myself to be an evangelist, small groups has always been more of a necessary chore than a great opportunity to me. It has always been difficult to get them going and even harder to keep them going. You are constantly required to police whatever book or study they're going through. Getting people to lead them or host them has always been hard. Often, people don't like others in their group and want to move or quit going all together. Many successful groups might tend to want to be exclusive. New people are not invited in and the group won't establish new leaders and new groups. Definitely out of my element, here I am in a church with over 800 small groups making it work without much concern at all for attraction.. As I recoiled from Jim's insistence on the primacy of discipleship, I felt myself continually backed into corners. "You're a flock shooter, Jerry," he said, evaluating the Crossing approach. "A flock shooter is a lousy hunter with a gun and no plan. When the flock is scared into flight, he just shoots as many rounds as he can into the flock hoping he'll hit something. Usually, he just wounds a few if he hits them at all. A good hunter picks out a bird, leads it, and pulls the trigger." He was saying that preaching to the crowd is like shooting the word of God into the congregation and hoping that you hit something. It wasn't the way that Jesus exampled or the way the early church operated. Again, Jesus got far more accomplished through 12 committed guys than he did with any of the large crowds he attracted. As Jim began to explain to me a different and better way of discipleship, I began to realize how we had missed the mark. In order for real discipleship to happen, there has to be three things present: An intentional leader, a relational environment, and a reproducible process.

An intentional leader is someone who has made it his business to reproduce disciples for Jesus. He does this more by watching and listening than by teaching. Jim compared this to a coach interacting with a player in practice, correcting him, watching him do it again and again, and adjusting and readjusting until the player is able to reproduce what the coach wants. The attractional model reduces potential players to spectators or fans coming out to watch the professionals play. Micropolitan communities are full of potential intentional leaders both inside and outside the church who have never been coached to coach.

A relational environment is one that allows the kind of individual attention to take place so that meaningful one-on-one dialogue can happen between a group member and a coach. Parents know that larger class sizes at school are never preferable because individual attention is critical for teachers to know the progress of their students. Small groups at Real Life work because they are relational environments where this intentional leadership and coaching can happen. The expectation is higher in a micropolitan community for individual attention. People in micropolitans do without metropolitan amenities because of their desire for a more tight knit culture.

A reproducible process is a means of coaching that makes the process of discipleship measurable. Having some sort of metric to track spiritual growth has been elusive in the church. We tend to put lots of options in front of a congregation and hope they find something that fits them that they can grow in. The process that Jim started at Real Life was revolutionary to me. He divides spiritual maturity into 4 phases. We renamed them to 1) accept, 2) belong, 3) care, and 4) disciple. Someone at the "accept" phase may or may not be a Christian. If they are, they are only attending as a spectator. Someone at the "belong" phase is involved in a relational environment (small group) and is starting the process of being coached by that group's intentional leader. Someone at the "care" phase is putting what he is learning to work in ministry. His small group is a place where he puts what he is learning into the context of his ministry and his intentional leader is looking for ways to move him into a coaching role. Someone at the "disciple" phase has become the intentional leader, reproducing what has been done in him and looking strategically at how to move individuals under his coaching forward. Notice that the word "phase" is used and not "level". The reason is because people need to be valued no matter which phase they are in. There will be some in the "accept" phase that will be far more effective in higher phases than many already there.

Coaching happens by listening to the questions and comments in the group and the coach driving the question or comment deeper into the person who gives it. As the person explores the comment on a deeper and more personal level, the coach is watching, listening, and getting a bead on the phase of his group member. Jim calls this "the phrase of the phase". A typical comment might be made about the story of Jesus washing Judas' feet. The group member might say, "I would never wash that jerk's feet!" (Accept level) He might answer, "It is so awesome that Jesus washed his feet!" (Belong level) He might say, "We all need to figure out ways to wash the feet of others." (Care level) Or he might say, "George, how does that hit you in the context of your divorce?" (Disciple level) The answers the coach hears will let him know what phase his people are in. That can't happen in a preaching environment.

The dialogue requires it to be relational. The leader is being intentional. His intention is figuring out where they are in order to move them forward. Look back at the "accept" phase answer. The coach would drive the comment back into the group member with something like, "When have you ever felt betrayed? How did you respond to it? How do feel about your response?" When one group member starts getting transparent, it gives the whole group freedom to open up. Before long, the intimacy level is rising and the coach is getting a great read of the phase of each group member.

This focus on discipleship closes the back door of the micropolitan church. As people move through "the dot", the reproducible process of discipleship transitions them from self-focused to others-focused. They don't leave because a new set of selfless priorities has replaced the set that attracted them. Further, there is a greater sense of unity that comes from alignment with the staff to meet the shared goals of growth in numbers and growth in maturity. Maturing Christians let personal wants take a back seat to whatever is most effective to get people through the sweet spot. The result is a healthy, growing, deepening, and unified body.

Part 3: Making It Work

The micropolitan model is more philosophy of ministry than practical application. The methods we use bring those philosophies to life in a real setting. This next section investigates "how" more than "why" in an effort to help establish or change parameters for effective ministry.

Visioneering

If the church is going to get any traction in becoming micropolitan, someone is going to have to cast a vision that the leadership, the staff, and the congregation can buy into. It has to be a vision that is God-given or people won't and shouldn't follow. It has to be a vision that makes sense because people can't follow what they can't understand. It has to be a vision that makes a big difference because passion and excitement is what fuels vision. It has to be a vision that is achievable because it will lose steam without clear progress. It has to be a vision that can be broken down into "wins" because progress needs to be measured.

The only person that can effectively cast such a vision is the lead pastor. He has to be the visioneer. As the lead communicator, he gives a voice to the vision. If the lead pastor doesn't have the ability to cast that vision effectively, the church needs to give up the idea of being micropolitan or they need to get a new pastor. Caution!!! As I said before, many churches don't have the stomach for change. I don't mean that they can't do meaningful ministry. I just mean that they will be doing it for a finite amount of time. Many pastors are just that…great pastors. They can preach and teach from God's word, visit the sick, and love people with the best of them…but they can't cast a vision. Without this ability and the confidence of his leaders, moving in this direction could be devastating to both the church and pastor. Visioneering requires alignment and a visioneering leader must have the support of his leadership. Leadership moves from the top down. I believe that if the pastor casts the vision and the leadership and staff move with it, the church will follow their unity.

When the Crossing decided to buy the community college campus, there were people who balked. Some wanted to concentrate on the failure of the past minister, some wanted to just go back and be what we were, and some were just sour to the idea. They needed someone in leadership who agreed with their negative point of view…a negative visionary so to speak. That was something they couldn't get. The vision for the Crossing that came from me to the elders was solid. They were all in. The elders of our church stood in front of the congregation after our weekend service as I shared the vision. Each one stood in turn and gave his reasons for the move. One elder had been coaxed to stand with the opposition. I will never forget him standing before the group and with tears streaming down his face sharing his passion for the lost. His testimony solidified the unity of the leadership and the faction who didn't want it soon dissipated. The vision and the alignment to that vision has remained a constant. It was the driving force behind our desire to launch multi-site campuses more than an hour away.

Visioneering requires redundancy. Leaders have to figure out ways to say it over and over again. Each time the church is reminded of the vision and the "wins" the church has experienced during the journey to achieve it, the vision is refreshed. Many of you have seen or have done cardboard testimonies as part of your worship services. If you haven't, just check out "cardboard testimonies" on YouTube. I remember just how effective of a tool that was to communicate our vision through the way that Jesus changes the lives of people who had found an intimate, personal relationship with Him. We extend our decision times to give people plenty of time to come forward and get on their knees, wash their hands in the water flowing over the baptistery, or find someone to pray with. They might come over to me to share something. I usually stand off to the side. The point is that everyone sees people all over the place doing business with God. It gives them permission to take action themselves and reminds them just exactly what we are all about. We video tape the baptisms at every service at every campus and play it back at every service. It only takes a couple of minutes but the reinforcement of the vision and the joy that is displayed is awesome! Like many churches, we take a series of sermons each year to realign our people to our vision, celebrate our wins, and redefine our purpose.

Remember, the vision never changes but there are always new means and methods that keep the dot dropping and the vision fresh. Visioneers are always hungry to find a new way of releasing that vision. When we listen to staff with an open and changeable attitude regarding means and methods, everybody wins.

Benchmark

Any visit to a metropolitan megachurch is a disheartening experience to a church leader from a micropolitan community. It begins with the parking lot. Just looking at the architecture says, "I can't do that!" I remember driving onto the campus of Willow Creek the first time. There was a beautiful diamond pattern on the manicured lawn. A picturesque lake reflected the beautiful building in the morning sun. The closer I drove, the better it looked. I walked through the doors into a light-filled atrium with coffee bar, food court, and upstairs bookstore all set against a wall of glass. There wasn't a stain to be found on the floor. People were sitting in comfortable conversation areas, drinking designer coffees and talking. Some were reading or working on their laptop. There were small groups seated at tables set for eight with their bibles open in front of them. It was awesome! It felt like community! The gap between this and what I would go home to was getting wider and wider. The diamond shaped auditorium had glass on two sides. Motorized shades came down to dim the room for the worship experience. I sat in my comfortable theater chair as I scanned their bulletin. Their *weekly* financial need was twice my *annual* church budget. The technology looked something like the bridge of the starship Enterprise. The bar was very high.

Well that was there…not in my little town. There were a number of things I could learn from this church that I could incorporate into mine without breaking the bank. The fact was, even small inexpensive changes would set us apart in Quincy. Going to a megachurch and adapting what we learn there is something we call benchmarking. Benchmark churches have come up with so many creative things that a micropolitan church can adapt and use for its target. When our church was running 500 in attendance, I planned a trip to Indianapolis and scheduled to visit four churches that ran between 1000 and 2500 for benchmarking. They were happy to take an hour or so out of their day to do what we asked. First, we wanted a tour of their building. A tour allows you to see how another set of creative minds do ministry. The size of the church is important as monster megachurches are so far removed in size that practical applications and adaptations might be difficult. These were just right. All sorts of ideas and discussions were born just out of those tours. Second, we scheduled one hour to sit down with our counterpart and ask specific questions about ministry approach. After our meetings, our team would get together and talk about what had inspired them. Changes on our campus came quickly after that. Doing this as a team was also critically important as it is hard to communicate something that someone else hasn't seen. It's that "You had to be there" syndrome.

It was incredible what something as simple as black paint did. Painting the ceiling black made it disappear, giving the feel of an auditorium. Painting the stage black made the worship leaders and band pop visually. Leaving a square of white and framing it in the middle of the back wall for projection cost nothing. Great projectors are only a couple of thousand dollars. Par cans aren't very expensive either. There was a whole group of technically savvy people in the church who finally had a place to honor the Lord with their passion. Comfortable stackable chairs allowed us to change seating configurations.

The impact of just seating configurations, the auditorium style, some well-placed lighting, and projection technology will immediately set a church in a micropolitan area apart. It's as much about what goes out the door as what comes in. Getting rid of the pulpit takes away a division from preacher to congregation. It gives an air of vulnerability and approachability. Losing the communion table and chairs says that communion is more about looking inward instead of how it's administered.

Jim Collins relates a story about a Brazilian company looking to pick the brains of American company CEO's involved in a similar business as theirs. Ten requests were made but only one CEO responded to the idea: Sam Walton. The Brazilian executives flew to Bartlesville, Oklahoma and were met with the famous pickup truck complete with Sam and his dog. They had lunch at his nondescript house that concluded with Sam washing the dishes in the kitchen sink. While he was washing the dishes, Sam began probing the Brazilians with questions about their business, their culture, their approach, and their goals. The point is that Sam wasn't entertaining these guests just to impart his Wal-Mart wisdom. He was learning. He was always looking for opportunities to learn how to do business better knowing that those revelations come from unlikely places. Great leaders love learning and one of the best ways to learn is to discover successful models and adapt their ideas. The whole purpose of this book is an attempt to throw the Crossing's hat into the arena of ideas. Who knows how many conversations will come from it that will give more traction to the cause of Christ?

Break Out of the Pack

If you do something outrageous in a micropolitan community, people will notice. Just because you have a building doesn't mean you have to meet in it for worship. I know that sounds silly but it speaks volumes to the 80% when you are willing to go to a secular environment, setting up and tearing down equipment each week just to get to know them. We are presently working with a secular location for a new work in Burlington, Iowa. It's the convention center at Catfish Bend Casino. Now the first questions some would be likely to ask would have something to do with a church being in a casino. It might offend churchgoers but it would certainly be interesting to the 80%! Since they are the target, it works perfectly. Just imagine all the free press! The Burlington idea is a great example of breaking out of the pack by being willing to do something that no other church would even consider.

There are some great models of mobile church out there. You might want to check out Lifechurch.tv or seacoastchurch.

com for some awesome insights into technology, children's areas, and other information. Our local paper has done scores of articles on our church. It happens every time we do something outrageous…like when we gave everyone ten bucks and told them to invest it God's kingdom…or the time we cancelled worship and organized an outdoor memorial day service at the local veterans home…or the time we started a high school party alternative to help stop under age drinking… or when we opened our thrift store…or gave all the children who couldn't afford them backpacks for school…you get the picture. Micropolitan communities are small enough to feel it when we reach out. The 80% see churches as spiritual fortresses with high walls. We want to show them that we are missionally mobilized members of their community.

The Crossing opened a second campus in Quincy with the specific mission of benevolence in mind. We moved completely out of our norm to purchase a 140-year-old church building in a residential area rampant with drugs, alcohol, and crime. Initially, we wanted to use part of the building as a residential addiction discipleship program for men. We also had plans for Celebrate Recovery, a soup kitchen, a benevolence triage program, and a ministry for single moms. We also planned to use the auditorium for an extension of our services. When the neighbors heard about our in-house recovery program, they balked. We were all over the local media as the church that was trying to do something for the addiction problems in the community and how a showdown was brewing between our prospective neighbors and us. We held an informational meeting to hear their questions, comments, and concerns. They all were happy with us coming into their neighborhood with our other ideas, but the addiction program was going to be a fight. The last thing we wanted to do was alienate the community we were trying to help so we took the proposal off the table. The neighbors appreciated being heard. We now have a campus in the heart of a hurting community ministering in all sorts of ways. Since that time, three businessmen have stepped up to build a new facility for the in-house recovery need on our original campus. These and other efforts make the Crossing stand out in our micropolitan community. They give us the opportunity to build trust and be considered a partner to make our city a better place to live without compromising our gospel message.

Keep a Balance

Engaging the 80% requires keeping a balance between purity and proximity. Jesus prays about His followers being in the world but not of it in John 17:14-18, but putting that concept into practice is a truly difficult thing in the church. Purity without proximity is judgmental, separatist, sheltered, and conceited. It becomes a hotbed for self-righteousness and finger pointing. Churches bent in this direction love to curse the darkness and talk about the good old days with longing affection. These churches may try to satisfy the requirement of proximity by being a "sending" church. "Sending" might be defined as a predominately traditional church that is comfortable with the usual. It is a predictable congregation committed to taking care of its own needs and giving to established mission works. They fulfill the obligation of proximity from a distance with their checkbook.

A church that practices proximity without purity is indistinguishable from the rest of the world. They really have nothing spiritual to offer as they have sacrificed life change for worldly relationships. Many of today's megachurches have resorted to proximity tactics like shock to bring in an audience. One church printed billboards advertising a sermon series called "My Lousy Sex Life". XXX church.com interfaces their parachurch ministry with churches using a program called "Missionary Positions". While these and other provocative ideas might attract people, tongue in cheek phrases might blur the line so much between the spiritual and worldly that the unchurched won't be able to distinguish a difference. Some might water down clear teachings from God's Word in an effort to bridge the gap. Paul admonishes us in Romans 14:22, *"Blessed is the man who does not condemn himself by what he approves."*

This tension between purity and proximity reveals itself in our personal lives as well. Some choose home schooling their children in an effort to protect their purity while others send their children to public school with an expectation that they will shine their light and influence the culture around them. Within this tension lie our movie and entertainment choices, our spending priorities, our closest friendships, and our time commitments. Many Christians have found their best solution in pretending…by acting one way in church environments and another in our social or work life. This solution neither honors God nor fools the world.

Jesus taught about this tension and reactions to both His and John the Baptist's ministry in Luke 7:31-35. When John came on the scene, his no-compromise approach directed listeners to repentance, striking a chord of revival in their hearts. He established proximity by the power of his message as people flocked to him. While sinners came to John, Jesus came to sinners. He calls Matthew from his tax-collecting table, Zacchaus from his tree, Simon from his boat, and Lazarus from his grave. He never compromises purity in His proximity. Even so, the perceptions of some were skewed.

To me, the most perfect picture of the balance between purity and proximity is Jesus on the cross. It reminds me of the time I was standing in the Sistine Chapel looking at the famous depiction in the center of the ceiling. Both God and Adam are reaching out for each other with a small-unpainted space between their outstretched fingers. Jesus closed that gap on the cross, one hand nailed in the direction of God, and the other in the direction of man. I see Him there with His body in tension, holding two worlds together in proximity and purity.

As the micropolitan church breaks out of the pack in pursuit of the 80%, it must remain ever mindful of this tension and keep a balance. We must remember that God's perception is the one we must be concerned about. We must avoid lazy ways of building proximity at the expense of purity as we venture out into the deep water of our culture.

Streamline Decision-Making

Churches regularly wrestle with the speed and agility they lack in the area of decision-making. This is especially true with churches that are not exclusively staff led that utilize a church board. Everyone has an opinion, some informed and some uninformed. Staff members or lay leaders are no different. Everyone fits in the body of Christ but Paul teaches us that our location and function in that body vary. There are just some things that others do better than us and vise-versa. There's nothing wrong with that...as long as everybody knows that depending on the subject, some leader's opinions are more informed and gifted than others. God designed the church to run more like an organism than an organization. Just like the human body, Christ expects His body, the church, to operate each according his gifts and abilities. The problem is that in the church, decision-making is often accomplished by committee after hearing each opinion equally. This may sound fair but isn't the way Christ designed the church to operate. Leaders rarely get to shine as brightly as they should because everyone wants to weigh in on the subject. Not only is the process slowed down, it is confused by opinions that aren't beneficial to the body moving forward.

In an effort to get a laser focus on this, we did a leadership exercise early on at the Crossing. Before our annual strategic leaders retreat, I asked each elder to write down what he saw as the greatest strengths of the others there. Those papers were turned in to me ahead of the retreat in order to be compiled. At the retreat, we had the elders sit in a circle, put a chair in the middle of the room, and one by one, had each elder sit in the chair. Once seated, I read to each elder what had been written about him. It was wonderful and humbling. After the comments were read, all the leaders gathered around him and prayed. Each elder broke down as he humbly received the praise. There were two very important things that became apparent through the exercise. First, they could see that in one or two areas, each leader was especially gifted. They began to realize that they had a specific role inside the leadership and that their opinion was vital in those specific areas. This didn't mean that their opinion in their weaker areas were useless, it just meant that God had provided the more gifted opinion from another person on the team. Working like an organism instead of an organization would make decisions come more quickly and would affirm each leader's contribution. The second revelation was that God had given us great talent in nearly every necessary area when we viewed ourselves as a body instead of a committee. It was awesome to see that God had already provided all we needed to make great, highly competent decisions. Discussion also streamlined as each leader gave the weight of opinion to the one with the recognized expertise. John Wooden, the great basketball coach, was often heard saying, "Be quick, but don't hurry!" Operating as a body makes the church quick to move, to pivot, to adjust, to release resources, and to trust each other while they do it. It accomplishes this without feeling frantic as deadlines approach, or feeling insecure because insufficient time was spent on a particular subject.

Finally, we gave each other the freedom to fail. In the church, there are failures and then there are failures. Moral failures involving sexual misconduct or misappropriation or use of money are epic. Failures in these areas can negatively redefine the church and handicap its future for years. The church must have safeguards in place so that leaders can't even get close to them. The failures I'm referring to are attempts to do ministry that fall apart because they were bad ideas or decent ideas that were executed poorly. There have been plenty of times that we've attempted an idea only to have it blow up in our face! It's not terribly important if it fails, it's what we do after the failure that will be most important.

Let's face it…if we try new things, we're not going to have a perfect record. In the micropolitan church, a steady supply of new ideas and approaches will be tried…and some will fail. Micropolitan leaders have to have the freedom to attempt things that may not work. When it became clear that The Crossing needed more worship space, we enlisted the help of a local architectural firm to do our drawings. We insisted that our top dollar for the project was 3 million dollars. We were repeatedly reassured that our financial ceiling was in no danger. When the bids finally came in, the average price tag was in the neighborhood of 6 million dollars. Adding insult to injury, the firm billed us $250,000.00 for drawings of a building too expensive for us to build. I think this would qualify as a failure. Instead of losing our composure, we adapted the plans using part of the plans and exchanging our fancy building for a pre-engineered steel building. The result was a great building that was done earlier than expected and well under our original budget. We failed but we failed together and we failed forward.

Sometimes, ideas might look like failures but just need a little more time. The Crossing decided that a Saturday evening service might reach a new group of people in the community. It didn't take off right away. We tried to enhance the service with food. We tried to make fellowship more special. We tried to encourage Sunday attenders to try it. Some were ready to give up on it as it was a drain on volunteers and resources. There were a lot of reasons to give up. We stuck with it and today it is as vibrant as the rest of our experiences.

Create a Culture of Change

A micropolitan church needs to experience change in small increments especially on the front end because each "win" increases the tolerance to change. As the church stacks up the "wins", it gains confidence and boldness to approach new ideas with enthusiasm instead of fear. The volume of previous successes creates a resistance to costs the occasional failures. Change in a church is like a bank account. Each "win" is a deposit and the costs in resources and people are the withdrawals. Failures are also a withdrawal. Managing change is making sure that the church isn't overdrawing their account.

Resistance to change comes from a number of different areas. The primary one that all churches in micropolitan communities are familiar with has to do with the cultural inertia that is always there. "We've never done it that way before" is a mantra inside their churches. The threat of losing people is a second source of resistance. Leaders don't like the thought of losing fellowship with people who have history in the church and worry about how the church might do without their money or involvement. A third resistance comes from a desire to be true to the faithful people who have entrusted the care of the church into the present leaders hands. The financial, social, and perceived spiritual implications of change are daunting.

Churches that want to go "micropolitan" need to strategically think about ways to lower resistance to change and raise levels of confidence. As discussed earlier, resistance to change is lowered when small successes are stacked up. Resistance is lowered when the right people are in favor of the change. Even though the pastor is the visionary, one of the key reasons for the necessity of lay leaders is to give credibility to the vision. Congregational members can marginalize the pastor's desire for changes, considering him to be a hired hand possibly influenced by his desire for personal success at the church's risk. They might question his motives, thinking that if his grand idea damages the church, he can just go elsewhere. When respected leaders who are part of the mosaic of the community unify with the pastor's vision, they give credibility the vision and resistance is lowered. A third way resistance is lowered is when the church is trying to reverse a downward spiral. A crisis may not be a great experience, but it is a powerful environment for change. Changes are dangerous in these times because the church is in a weakened state, but if it is in a desperate time, desperate measures might be necessary. It's been said, "Never waste a good crisis!"

The Crossing was in a crisis in 1998 when the pastor left after a moral failure. Attendance dropped by 100, nearly a third of the total number at that time. Leadership focus was in the rear view mirror as the pieces of a shattered vision were lying all around them. The purchase of a community college campus was not a small change. Change is always better in small increments, but desperate times called for desperate measures. The risks were very high but the need for a new vision and desperate feeling that the crisis created lowered resistance. It wasn't just a novel idea as the elders really felt the presence and direction of God in the move. The unity of the leadership in the purchase of the campus gave the new vision credibility and resistance to change continued to lower. As the church grew, the "wins" developed confidence in the vision and the leaders. Today, the Crossing has great agility to change because it maintains a very high balance in the bank account...not with money but with confidence. The congregation embraces new approaches because the "wins" have greatly reduced their fears.

In 2009, The Crossing was faced with a failure I will discuss in the multi-site section of this book. Three of our five staff members left in one of our locations. There was no doubt that this failure made a big withdrawal in our confidence account. With the perfect storm of financial vulnerability brought on by stretching out into a new community, making a poor decision on a campus pastor, and the financial meltdown of the national economy, our leaders lost a good portion of their confidence to take risks. Even though the recovery came quickly with the location rebounding with staff and attendance in about 4 months, the sting of that failure lingered. During the experience, Nathan, our multi-site discipleship pastor gave me a little book to read I referred to earlier. It was *How the Mighty Fall* by Jim Collins. I could clearly see my error in the second step of capitulation, "hubris brought on by success". I had developed so much confidence in our model that I became arrogant and cut corners in the hiring process. I didn't think it was possible for our model to fail. Dependence on God for wisdom had quietly been replaced with arrogance. I look back at the experience and consider it failing forward. While it was painful and took its toll on the church's confidence account, God also used it to prepare our hearts for greater things that would require a greater dependence on Him.

It is human nature to be change resistant but it gets easier when people are resigned to its necessity. Let's say you are working at your job and the boss comes in and says that as an exercise, he wants you to write your name with your left hand. (Assuming you are right-handed) Your signature probably looks pretty pathetic. Then he tells you that he wants you to write that way for the rest of the day. Uncomfortable as that might be, you might tolerate that. What if he said that he wanted you to write that way for a week, a month, or even a year? At what point would you find your breaking point and say, "That's enough! This is not the way I was designed. I'm much more comfortable using the hand I've always used!" That makes total sense if you have full confidence the status quo. But let's say that there is an accident and you've lost the use of your right hand or its function has been greatly reduced. Even though mechanically it's going to be just as difficult as the exercise the boss wanted, the perception of the change is going to be completely different, making the acceptance of the new behavior easier. Now, each time the awkward action is repeated, it becomes a little less awkward. While change is never really easy, it is going to be much more palatable in a culture of change.

Empower Volunteers

I believe micropolitan people are more community-minded and work harder to hold their communities together than metropolitan people. Why? It's all part of the texture of a micropolitan community. People are closer knit. These people like knowing the name of the cashier at their favorite grocery store. They like being on a first name basis with the high school principal. They sign up for the PTO or the Pinewood Derby. People who live in urban or suburban areas are more disconnected from the diversity of their social context. With job security at an all-time low and corporate buy-outs and reorganizations the norm, people can't help from keeping the social root system shallow. While this context has its advantages and disadvantages, the micropolitan context tends to be more stable. Social ties are so strong and such a priority that the families who live in them will make drastic economic adjustments to stay. In the 1970's, Motorola closed it's Quincy plant, displacing 3,000 employees in a town of 40,000. While this was economically devastating, the city reorganized itself from a manufacturing town to a more service oriented community. Most of those employees adapted to other employment or commutes in order to stay. Today the city is doing as well as well as it was back then, or perhaps better than ever.

Micropolitan people are pre-disposed to sign up and show up. They take ownership in what they are involved in and love doing it. While metropolitan churches are far more bent in the direction of paying for staff to cover ministry areas funded by wealthy donors, micropolitan people step up themselves. Their spirit of volunteerism is just part of the fabric of the community. Whether you look at little league, scouting, tutoring, service organizations, or big brothers and sisters, volunteers take ownership of the needs of their community. This is fertile ground for the volunteer structure necessary in a micropolitan church. I've had plenty of conversations from visitors who come from large cities who are mystified by how many volunteers we have at our campuses. We are capitalizing on one of the intrinsic benefits of being micropolitan.

The first requirement needed to develop a great volunteer base is simple grace. We give plenty of room for people to make mistakes. Have you ever seen and heard a church children's choir perform? One little girl always lifts up her dress, at least a couple frown and refuse to sing, some just aren't paying any attention at all, and one or two are singing loud enough for the whole choir. Have you noticed the parents and grandparents? They don't care at all. Video cameras are rolling, smiles are from ear to ear, and ovations are always standing. Why? It's because *who they are* is more important than *what they're doing*. Micropolitan communities have a lot more room for that kind of grace. They know that the person singing or running lights is their neighbor who works at the local hospital or factory. They can see the "*who*" as much as the "*what*".

The second requirement in raising up volunteers is setting them up for success by balancing excellence with empowerment. Commonly we give ministry over to a volunteer by getting them to say yes and then handing them their tools and a schedule. Without proper training we are setting them up for failure. A volunteer gets exposed to a ministry area in stages. It begins with low impact involvement like parking cars or handing out bulletins. In children's areas, it might just be observation or helping in preparation without direct interaction. As they acclimate, we praise their contribution and challenge them to take another step forward. In the lobby, this might look like a floating problem solver, helping people check in, drop off their kids, find a good seat, or take a tour of the church. Now the volunteer is engaging others in conversation. In a small group, it might look like providing a host home. Responsibility increases with excellence and the success empowers the volunteer to entertain other areas of ministry. Our volunteers are constantly moving and exploring. The Crossing has shattered the 80/20 rule by giving ministry away; balancing excellence with empowerment in the micropolitan setting. Each week at the Crossing, hundreds of people put on their nametags and smiles and help make church happen. We couldn't do it without them.

Hire Micropolitan

While micropolitan communities may be great places to raise families and grow churches, they don't tend to be magnets for ministry professionals. Those who are highly gifted tend to look for roles in metropolitan or suburban settings. For many, a smaller setting is viewed as career suicide. So how does a micropolitan church compete for the best and brightest to be in their dugout? Here are some great ideas that have made the difference for us:

Hiring from Within

Not everyone who enters ministry feels called before the age of 18, but the church relies heavily on Bible colleges, Christian colleges, or seminaries to provide for their professional needs. For the most part, the church has generally abdicated her responsibility to raise up those professionals to the halls of higher education. In most churches, the best biblical education one can get is going to come out of a Sunday School class or a small group. Any church educational program is going to be inferior to what goes on at college. Like the rest, our church had no systematic plan of study for education let alone a path that incorporated that study into practical use. Many who have come to Christ at the Crossing, find Him after normal college years. They are in the midst of a career with a spouse and children, a mortgage, and a dog. Conventional college just isn't practical anymore. Some have opted for online opportunities offered by some schools. While this is an option, the costs are highly prohibitive. When credit hour costs hover somewhere between $400 to $800 per hour, it certainly makes this kind of opportunity a pipe dream for many.

It has always frustrated me that it costs so much for people to learn God's Word at this level. I think that it is the responsibility of the church to "teach them all that I have commanded you". Some of the church's greatest waste is in the human capital that God provides but we fail to use to their greatest potential. Out of that frustration, Ministry Development Institute was conceived.

Ministry Development Institute is a tool that the Crossing has created to develop people that God has raised up internally for ministry. It takes its cues from the way Jesus made leaders.

At least 11 of the 12 apostles were outsiders to prevailing religious culture. They were for the most part uneducated and unconnected. After Jesus had ascended to heaven, the Jerusalem religious leaders were amazed at the knowledge and courage of the apostles, realizing they were "unschooled, ordinary men". (Acts 4:13) While they were outsiders to religious pedigree, they were insiders to Jesus. "They took note that they had been with Jesus" is what Luke's account explains. While they didn't have a formal education in the conventional sense, they had the invaluable resource of being with Jesus day and night for 3 years.

Like this biblical illustration, there are people within our churches with incredible potential that have completely bought in to the church's DNA and approach. They don't need to be convinced or taught how we reach out or do ministry, they just need to couple it with some formal education to put some credibility with their ministry. Who would have picked Simon Peter for the inaugural leader of first century Christianity? Who would pick someone with a resume' like Matthew to be a biographer for Jesus? This makes me think about God calling an 80-year-old Moses out of exile to deliver His people out of Egypt. When Moses questions God's call by asking, "What if they do not believe me or listen to me and say, "The Lord did not appear to you?" God's response was simple. He asked, "What is that in your hand?" Maybe we should be asking the same question. Maybe God has already resourced us with much of the human capital we need. Like Jesus, we just need to unlock their potential by coupling their desire with great training.

I met Jim in 2002 when he moved back to town and started attending the Crossing. He was making a six-figure salary working as a regional sales manager for a national company. He had a business degree from SMU and had owned or run businesses over the years. In his mid-forties, success was starting to give way to a desire for significance. He had been a high functioning alcoholic for many years and was in recovery. His past addiction and lifestyle had blown him through a lot of money and three marriages. I would never have guessed that he would give it all up for a chance at ministry. Jim runs Celebrate Recovery and the Crossing 929 campus.

Chris was managing a local restaurant. A drug-addicted wife whom he had divorced had complicated his life, but he continued to raise their two children. He met his present wife while they were both employed at the restaurant. She encouraged him to go church with her but he put up a fight. God's plans for him were different than running a restaurant. Chris is a children's minister at the Crossing today.

Pam was working at CarQuest Auto Parts. Now she runs our front office. Joe graduated form Truman State University and managed political campaigns before taking a job managing an interactive website and online components for a medical school. Now he pastors youth at our Kirksville campus. These are a few of our staff members and students of Ministry Development Institute. They are only a few of the internal hiring we have done. MDI gives us a tool to give an education that is nearly equivalent to a Bible college.

MDI is the brainchild of Dr. Alan Rabe, a Crossing church member who used to be the dean of the graduate school of Hope International University. He shared my passion for raising up ministry professionals and servant leaders from within the church. He has developed a plan of study that takes 18 months, incorporating emphasis in Old and New Testament, interpretation, and application. What does it cost? The 18-month course of study costs $240 for the entire thing. What is the time requirement? It is a 3-hour class that meets once a week with integrated online discussion and homework. MDI gives a high level of competency to people that God might raise up from within the church to pursue a more comprehensive path of Biblical knowledge. Whether that is released professionally in a hired position or used in volunteer ministry, MDI drives spiritual roots down deep. We divide classes into groups of 12 at a time. Those 12 stay with each other through the entire learning experience. We began offering MDI to staff only, then branched out into elders, volunteer ministry leaders, and church members.

I can hardly wait to see how MDI affects the ministry of this church long term. It has increased our staffing options exponentially. It is my hope that our success would serve as a template for other churches who wish to pick up the responsibility of educating their leaders found within their walls to greater levels of understanding and more effective ministry.

Hiring Externally

The Crossing's DNA is non-negotiable in the most critical hires. It's not that other ways aren't valid for ministry, but our model just requires a high level of alignment in order to be successful. We have always tried to look at relocating present staff when launching a new campus knowing that a common understanding of "our way" was absolutely critical for success. The one time that we deviated from this path was nothing short of disastrous for us. But moving people into new locations would stretch our staff sometimes to the point of breaking. Trying to hire from other churches also didn't work well for us not only because of alignment differences, but also big gaps in compensation. Most other churches pay more than we do and we couldn't compete financially. Those we have hired from other churches have had to endure substantial pay cuts to work on our team. One thing good about that is that we weed out people who choose ministry as a "career". We prefer to hire those who feel a "calling". I'm not saying that people accustomed to making more money aren't called but I have seen a substantial increase in Bible college students looking at ministry more as a job or career.

The Crossing likes to partner with people who see what they do more as mission than ministry. A missionary embraces all sorts of potential barriers to follow his calling. Financial support, language and cultural differences, inadequate resources and facilities, and little or no structure are the norm on the mission field. We consider our micropolitan approach missional. In my limited knowledge of the term "missional", it has seemed to me that it is often defined in the context of less people. Emphasis on the casual conversation at the coffee shop, the house church, or the random act of kindness seems more of an abandonment of organized thinking and approach for a "do your own thing" mentality. I understand the concept of getting beyond the walls of the church to minister to people where they live, but we have so much more potential impact when we exploit the strength of our numbers and unity. With 2/3 of our public decisions being first time, we certainly do not reflect the primary transfer growth of many American churches. While the areas we concentrate on are not completely unchurched, they are certainly underchurched. Our emphasis on benevolence and addiction recovery adds to this. The poor and the addicted are not usually big givers so money is in shorter supply. Less money means more creative thinking and adaptation. The problem remains of how to find and develop a staff that you know shares your DNA, is highly gifted in their area of ministry, and can be brought on staff without breaking the bank.

There are great biblical illustrations for hiring externally as well. The apostle Paul was the consummate insider to professional Judaism but a complete outsider to the church. As a Jew with Roman citizenship and the training of their best Rabbi, Gamaliel, Paul was on his way to superstardom in Judaism. He was a persecutor of the church until Jesus redirected his life on the road to Damascus. As a Christian evangelist, he had access to areas of ministry that others could only imagine, but to the church, he remained an outsider. It took someone like Barnabas to build bridges between Paul and the new Christian leaders. In time, they were able to direct his formal education and gift of persuasiveness to the establishment of churches all over the known world. And who went with Paul as he started on his venture? Barnabas. The insider stayed alongside the outsider until there was no further doubt that Paul was the real deal.

The way the Crossing has dealt with hiring externally is by creating a farm league. Our farm league consists of interns that we hire for a 6-month period to learn from a staff leader in a specific area of ministry. We concentrate in five areas: campus leadership, worship, youth, discipleship, and tech. Youth is broken down into student, children, and early childhood. These interns have already received the majority of their formal education, however, they lack an understanding of the Crossing's specific DNA and ministry approach. Our desire is to couple what they already have with what they will need for successful ministry alongside of us. We pay our interns $100 a week, provide them with a host home, and expect a 6-month commitment. Those who wish to be on our farm league apply with us and are interviewed. Our farm league seasons are from January to mid-June and from mid-June to mid-December. We presently bring on 7 interns per year. Initially, we recruited them, but now they seek us out. For the equivalent of the salary of a single starting staff member, we get 7 full-time employees. Comparing hour to hour, we might not be getting as much, but we are trading 40 hours for 280! Our investment and coaching can bring a sharper focus on our DNA, our mission, and our vision to our interns. We have the opportunity to observe them over a substantial period of time in a controlled environment where expectations are lower. We can see if they have the necessary buy-in for our vision, the proper chemistry for our staff, passion for our approach, the gifts to make a difference, and the character to hold it together. We learn if they could be comfortable in a micropolitan, and have a great source for hiring in the future for new or existing campuses. There really isn't a downside. If they don't work out or keep our internship rules, it's not terribly painful to let them go. Since most Bible college students require an internship as part of their requirements for their degree, we have a constant supply of candidates. If we do choose to hire, the negotiation and hiring process is easy and we are able to use our precious staff dollars to their greatest effect. Without a process like this, it would be virtually impossible for us to continue to look at new Crossing locations.

Hiring Family

A third well that the Crossing draws from is one that most intentionally avoid. The Crossing breaks "conflict of interest" rules on a regular basis. Most businesses have rules to protect them from the potential sticky situations that may result from hiring family or close friends. The Crossing considers this a risk we are willing to take. Many hiring opportunities are lost to micropolitans because the community doesn't have nearly as many amenities as the big cities and surrounding areas. Since so much of America is moving in the direction of urbanization, church professionals might look at metropolitan environments as places where their impact would have the greatest effect. The church financial picture appears slimmer in most micropolitans even though it might be made up in cost of living. This too may make the consideration of a micropolitan less attractive. For these and other reasons, churches struggle as "good fits" for many highly gifted professionals. The Crossing has taken advantage of the relationships it's staff has with relatives and friends to hire out of those pools. Since we generally hire younger people in keeping with our desire to keep "the dot" low, many are single and find their mates in the communities they serve. That keeps them from moving. Since we hire family members, it creates inertia for them to stay as they enjoy the proximity of the relationship.

When I ministered in west central Indiana, I had a farmer friend who worked with his father and brother. There were days when he was nearly suicidal because of how they would drive each other crazy, but most days he loved it. He used to say that working with family meant higher highs and lower lows. I think there is great wisdom in that thought. If we can be up front with the potential negative issues that can arise, and they will arise, we can dip into a well of great potential for the church. You'll notice that there was a lot of nepotism around Jesus. Most of his closest relationships were people who were either related to Him or each other. It would have been a shame for Jesus to say yes to Peter but no to Andrew, yes to John and no to James. No one would think of disqualifying John the Baptist simply because he was Jesus' cousin. The Crossing has hired wives, husbands, brothers, sisters, parents, best friends, and so on. We've hired elders into paid staff positions. We are careful in the vetting process, realizing that sometimes the dynamics in some relationships would not work or are too dangerous, but we enjoy the freedom and opportunity to hire inside these relationships with the absence of disqualifying policies.

Part 4: Teaching Old Dogs New Tricks

In the course of the history of the Crossing, there has been a number of what Henry Blackaby calls "crisis of beliefs". These forks in the road and the decisions that go with them redefine us personally. Blackaby's teaching is sobering. He relates, "When God tells me what He wants to do through me, I will face a crisis of belief." His statement is made as a forgone conclusion: not up for debate. It is a crisis because the things God calls us to are God-sized and require faith. He continues with an even more sobering statement, "What you do in response to God's revelation reveals what you believe about God." He defines faith as "the confidence that what God has promised or said will come to pass". He then connects the personal experience with how it plays out in ministry. "Our world is not seeing God because we are not attempting anything that only God can do. Let the world see God at work and that will attract people!" These teachings coming from his book *Experiencing God* are some of the most personally powerful that I have ever experienced in my life! Taking these concepts into my heart and life is what God used to change the way I approached my mission. He took me from leading a church of 300 to leading a church of nearly 4000…from managing a staff of 2 to over 50…from one location to multiple locations…from local to international.

Robert Frost's timeless poem is a perfect picture of my life and all those who don't resign themselves to the usual.

Two roads diverged in a yellow wood,
And sorry I could not travel both
And be one traveler, long I stood
And looked down one as far as I could
To where it bent in the undergrowth;

Then took the other, as just as fair,
And having perhaps the better claim
Because it was grassy and wanted wear,
Though as for that the passing there
Had worn them really about the same,

And both that morning equally lay
In leaves no step had trodden black.
Oh, I marked the first for another day!
Yet knowing how way leads on to way
I doubted if I should ever come back.

I shall be telling this with a sigh
Somewhere ages and ages hence:
Two roads diverged in a wood, and I,
I took the one less traveled by,
And that has made all the difference.

Like my personal story, the church stands at Robert Frost's fork in the road again and again. On the one side, the path is familiar and predictable. The other is neither, but when we take the necessary risks for impact by getting outside of our desire for personal comfort, the invisible God becomes more visible to us as we find ourselves leaning on Him often in desperation. The success or failure of any church is based on how they handle the crisis of belief. God **will** confront His church over and over with things he wants to see accomplished. He won't leave these challenges for us to figure out by ourselves.

The church is His responsibility. If we don't sense our church regularly in a crisis of belief, I would have to question whether God is still working through the church. We shouldn't have an expectation that God would do anything fresh in the church if we say no to the unpredictable path never previously taken. It has to be something the church would be incapable of doing without supernatural intervention so that it can't be confused as the result of purely human effort. God's purpose in this is much more than just the fulfillment of a mission. He wants us to experience His own unmistakable power and presence.

The micropolitan church throws its arms around these game-changing experiences. We don't want to waste our time attempting things that anyone could do. We want the supernatural presence of God to be the norm. We want to be the church where people come to see God at work. We want our willingness to accept the challenges that God puts before us to reveal that our dependence on Him is more than lip service.

Churches in micropolitan communities that resist these challenges may not truly want to honor traditions as much as hide behind them. There is another truth that Blackaby relates in his book. It is that unbelief is very costly. I once heard a parable that illustrated this truth.

A Christian man died and went to heaven. He found himself before heaven's gates and walked through them. Jesus was waiting for him on the other side. The man was overwhelmed with wonder and love as Jesus took his hand to share what He had prepared for His child. Then Jesus said that before He showed him into his new home, He had something he wanted to share with him. Reaching behind a curtain, Jesus pulled out a huge work of art. It was a charcoal rendering on paper displaying scene after scene in black, white, and various shades of gray. As the man looked closer, he could see that the images captured on paper were all scenes from his life. They were all the moments where he had honored his Heavenly Father and brought fame to the name of Jesus. Scene after scene washed over his memory as he thought of Jesus, the Artist, recording them with His own hand in sweeping lines and shades. Words escaped him as he fumbled for words to voice his appreciation. Then Jesus said, "Before we go in, there's something else I want to show you." Once again Jesus reached behind the curtain only this time he pulled out a work of art much larger than before. Instead of paper, the larger surface was of stretched canvas. The scenes were captured in the vivid color and texture of oils. As the man attempted to take in the beauty of what Jesus had done, he noticed that the same scenes that he had seen on the previous work of art were there, but hundreds more were there that he neither remembered nor recognized. When he asked Jesus about the additional scenes Jesus replied, "This is what your life would have looked like if it had been fully surrendered to Me." And that was when Jesus wiped away the tears from his eyes. *WOW!!*

Too many times we let our unbelief get in the way of the wonderful things that God is wanting to do to us and through us. I remember the first time I traveled to Israel. One of the sights that surprised me was the Dead Sea. Growing up in church, I had a picture in my head of what it must look like. I imagined leafless trees with broken branches, the smell of rotting fish, and scum floating on the surface of the water. Nothing could have been further from the truth. It was the most pristine body of water I had ever seen. There was nothing dead or dying near it. It was then that it occurred to me that for something to die or decompose, it had to live first. The reason the Dead Sea is so pristine is because there is absolutely nothing living there. Without life there is no death or decay. The main reason for this is that the Dead Sea has no outlet. The Jordan River flows in but not out. Further north, the Jordan flows into the Sea of Galilee and then out as it goes south to the Dead Sea. The Sea of Galilee is teaming with life. On it's shore one can picture the apostle fisherman hauling in their miraculous catch of fish. Churches can be like those two bodies of water. We're so afraid of death that we banish life altogether. There is a huge cost to unbelief that often goes unnoticed in the church. Opportunities are lost and victories are never experienced when we choose not to listen to God moving us into a crisis of belief.

Anytime we are faced with a game-changer at the Crossing, we are going to lose people. Anything God-sized is going to take us out of our comfort zone. Remember the definition of leadership: "Leadership is making people uncomfortable at a rate they can tolerate." The micropolitan church is determined to stay uncomfortable. It has chosen experiencing Christ over comfort.

Debt

I am really reluctant to write this next section because I know that it flies in the face of so much teaching in the church today. We have all gotten a steady dose of Dave Ramsey and the late Larry Burkett on how to handle finances. The overarching statement derived from any time with these teachings is this: Debt is bad! I'm wondering how many people I would offend if I were to say, "Debt is good!". I don't think I'll venture that far into this mine field, but I will say that acquiring debt has definitely been a game-changer for the Crossing. I know that debt is considered a necessary evil and it's certainly no fun to fund huge interest payments, but it is also necessary to realize that there is a cost to doing business. When I look at the financial picture of the Crossing, I see many business costs and I don't consider building debt differently than other debt.

Statistically, about half of a church's income is used to pay its staff. It is by far the largest incurred cost at any church in America today. Let me ask you a question. Should the cost of having a staff be considered debt? If we make a commitment to hire, aren't we responsible to pay a debt for service rendered? The employee is in debt to the employer according to the agreement between them. The employer is also in debt to compensate the employee. If we overextend ourselves financially and try to compensate by reducing staff or laying them off, aren't we defaulting on a debt we've committed to? Having a staff is just part of doing business. Without them, there would be no way to accomplish the tasks that make us effective.

Our programming also has costs attached to it. There are materials that we furnish, utilities that we use, and supplies we go through. We want the building to be warm on cool days and cool on warm ones. We want to be able to flip a switch and have the light go on. We want to have a bulletin to pass out. All of these things cost something and in order to do business, they need to be provided. The reason that capital debt stands out is the interest attached to it. We look at the cost of interest and feel that we're just throwing the money away. If we could raise all of the money up front for a capital project, then we would have so much more money to spend. The problem is that we can't...not if we want to make the investment to attract the 80%. You would be hard pressed to find a church that is growing significantly that doesn't or hasn't incurred debt. Interest is just the cost of using someone else's money. The American economy is built and runs on it.

While I love to use Kingdom principles derived from the Bible and know that it is often quoted as a template for staying out of debt, but there are big differences between the Jewish and American economies. Jewish law used the tithe as a tax. The political and religious structures were connected. Jewish law placed limits on debt to 7 years and land laws respected only renting, as land would eventually revert to its original owner. These are just a few of the big differences. I have heard countless referrals to "the borrower is slave to the lender". It's true. However, it is also true that the lender is slave to the borrower if that's how the lender makes his living. If the apostle Paul would have waited till he had raised all the money he needed for his missionary journeys before he left, I wonder if he would have ever gotten out of Antioch.

The Crossing uses about 20% of its general fund to manage its debt repayment. Like any home or business, we don't want to get over our heads by leveraging too much of our funds to pay capital debt. However, we don't want to make being debt free our goal either. The man who had been entrusted with one talent hid it and gave it back to his master. The master expected that at the very least, he should have earned some interest with it. When the master received it back, he not only gave it to the man who had ten, he threw the other man out of his sight! Do we ever look positively at the man in the place of weeping and gnashing of teeth because he was debt free? I have no desire to focus on money any more than I have to focus on the building it provides.

God is looking for us to produce and multiply in His Kingdom but we must understand that His currency is people. Isn't it interesting that he gave the one talent to the servant who had ten? I think when it comes to the Kingdom of God, more is better. The effectiveness of the use of His resources is measured by the amount of people we influence for Him. The servant with ten did the most with what he had. I think God is interested in us doing the most with what we have.

If we can do that most effectively without incurring debt, great! I haven't figured that one out, especially when I am trying to grow by attracting the 80%. The 80% aren't predisposed to give. The Crossing sees giving lag around 18 months behind attendance. If our numerical growth slows down, our per capita giving goes up. If our growth increases, the opposite happens. Attraction is expensive and so is an outward missional focus. Churches that want to be micropolitan are going to have to find ways of funding the changes necessary to be attractive. While there are ways of doing it cheaper than megachurches in metropolitan areas, it can't be done for free. It requires forward-thinking leaders to step out into areas of faith in the acquiring and use of money. Without a vision and a leadership willing to stand up and make the hard decisions necessary to fund our approach, the Crossing would still be just another church in Quincy riding the attendance elevator up and down between 100 and 300. Negotiating for the purchase of the college campus with the debt we incurred changed our game.

How to Get a Loan

Banks make loans based on their certainty of being paid back with interest. Their financial interest is secured by the value of what they are financing. In church matters, that puts banks in a potentially bad position. Local banks want to be viewed as a part of the community that makes it better, funding projects that improves the quality of life while at the same time, turning a profit for their stockholders. This makes funding a church risky. Repossessing a church is really bad PR. Banks also don't really understand church giving dynamics. It can make the process of a loan difficult. Here are some possible steps in the right direction:

1. Have a great paper trail. If a church can show a healthy financial position, a history of giving, a plan for making timely payments, and a projection of growth. This will make a big difference to a loan official. Having a church leader that happens to be a gifted accountant has been a

great personal asset to me as I approach a game changer. It has always served to give me a good sense of the church's position and risk exposure. Since church boards will always question the financial sense of a pastor, a reputable leader that is conservative will really help create buy-in by leadership. Some denominations have internal funding agencies for church loans. The Crossing eventually moved our debt to one of these. They told us that they had never seen such detailed financials by a local church before.

2. Use relationships that already exist in the church. Every time we have secured a loan, we have known someone in the bank or someone who knows someone. Much of the business in banks is done inside established relationships between them and business/community leaders. Churches have access to some of these. Banks might ask for wealthier people to act as guarantors or cosigners of the loan. Until the church is more established, this may be necessary.

3. Get a substantial amount of the money for the project committed ahead of time. Like all loans, the better the down payment and income stream, the more confident the bank will be in the church's ability to keep their commitment to repay. With that being said, here are some ideas to raise money:

Fundraising in churches today really comes in two basic ways; capital campaigns and regular giving or tithing. I've worked with a number of companies that conduct capital campaigns and have done some just on our own. They are all basically the same. The actual goal is to enlist as many church people as possible in the actual process. If someone is on one of the various project committees, he or she is more likely to give as part of the project. Capital campaigns usually become the primary focus of a church for at least 4 or 5 months. There is an enlistment phase where leaders are assigned and the church is recruited to serve. It is followed by a working phase where committees plan advance commitment, various mailings, a brochure, a special all-church giving event, and follow-up. The "intensive period" is usually 4 weeks with sermons about pledging, testimonies sharing individual commitments, and a banquet where pledge cards are turned in. Companies provide a consultant representative who coaches enlistment, provides encouragement and templates for mailings and brochures, and just generally oversees the process. He is valuable, but expensive. The cost of a consulting firm is usually calculated against the size of the church. We paid about $45,000 as a church of less than 1,000 in attendance. The cost is incorporated into the project but it is by no means small. However, the fact is that the amount we've raised has always been substantially higher when using a consultant.

One thing to remember about capital campaigns...the hardest money to raise is the money you've already spent. People get excited about a new building or something they can see happening. They don't tend to get excited about debt retirement. Some pastors are great fundraisers and just love opportunities like this. I'm not one of them. I don't like telling a congregation how much I'm giving or the slick salesmanship associated with the process. I don't like making fundraising for a particular project a 4-5 month church focus, but I do love having the tools to make the vision happen. A three-year pledge will go a long way to make a bank feel more secure about loaning money to a church.

Teaching tithing and regular giving is the best way to handle the ongoing expenses of the micropolitan church. Tithing is one of the last things new believers commit to. One of the reasons for a lag in tithing is that it is such a foreign concept to the unchurched. Let's face it: a tithe is a substantial amount of money for anyone. Most people coming to Christ in their adult years don't have their lives set up to give like this initially. Median household income in our area is just under $40,000.00. That's about $750 a week or over $300 a month before taxes. That money will make a car payment or cover the grocery bill. Many of the people the Crossing attracts are not in the most stable time of their lives. Their finances may be complicated by child support, bad debt, legal trouble, school loans, and so forth. We attract the young disproportionably and they don't tend to have much in the way of disposable income. The Bible teaches us to trust God to take care of us and to show our dependence through the tithe, but a steady diet of preaching on giving will nix the idea that "All the church wants is my money!". It's a pretty big lifestyle change for someone new to Christ.

At the same time, it takes money to fund the game-changers the micropolitan church needs. I can't remember a time that the Crossing has been "comfortable" financially. While we have longed for that feeling, we also realize that it can be much more dangerous than being in need. I wish it wasn't the case that both individually and corporately we are more focused on the Lord when we are in need, but it seems that the greater the need, the tighter the focus. I think about the parable of the man who buried his talent. He never let that talent be at risk and gave it back as he had received it. The owner's response was harsh to say the least. God wants us to put what he entrusts to us at risk for a return. This keeps us in a constant state of dependence and need, but also in a place where the Kingdom is receiving a return. I tell people to be assured that if they give their money, we won't hold it, we'll spend it. We have often been criticized for "stealing sheep" from other churches. It is true that about 1/3 of our growth is people coming from other churches but I also see it as God moving His people to a place where their time, treasure, and talent is going to be reinvested into the Kingdom just like that one talent going to the one who had ten. We take usually 4 weeks each year to teach the Biblical concept of giving. We wrap it up in interesting ways to be sensitive to those who are new our church.

Facility

The micropolitan church attracts people by being counter-cultural. That means being what people don't expect. For a first impression, one of the most important ways this is accomplished is in the look and use of the facility. Just the fact that we bought a place that would have been hard to sell otherwise made it attractive. There was a sense of partnership with the community to take something they needed to sell and make it a jewel in the crown of the community. Our facility choice was a game-changer.

Good Buys

Our campus in Quincy was originally a black eye to the community. It was built to be the best and most beautiful educational environment in Quincy. No expense was spared. In 1970, it was a sight to behold. Its design won architectural awards. Its technology was unsurpassed. There was only one problem: the teaching technique it was designed and built after, the open-learning concept, soon fell out of favor and was abandoned for more conventional approaches. The building was abandoned with the concept but the increased taxes to cover the bill left the community wanting. After a few more years, a local community college decided to use the campus. Once again, a tax was leveraged to cover the cost. Now the community was paying for this white elephant a second time. When the college outgrew it, we came along.

Quincy appreciated not having to buy it a third time. Our deal with the community college allowed them to get 4 times its sale price in state matching funds. They built a beautiful campus just down the road. It is one of Quincy's greatest assets today. Our cooperation made all this possible. Since the building had been used by the public for years as both an elementary school and a college, they were comfortable coming into it. It wasn't perceived as a church.

People expect to see gabled roofs, a steeple, stained glass, pews, and all the other usual stuff of churches. They weren't to be found at the Crossing. Making the environment unexpected kept visitors off-balance. Removing their expectations left them open to something new. It is amazing how something as simple as a worship space can bring defenses down. Those people who had churchy expectations that we needed to meet in order to keep them were not the ones we were looking to attract. The counter-cultural approach has proved to be very productive for the 80%. It also opens up lots of existing vacant buildings as potential church sites. Micropolitan communities have some great options at bargain prices. When we looked at the community college in Quincy, we initially thought that a purchase was out of reach, but because the school was so motivated by promise of matching funds, they bent over backwards to make it work for us.

The building we purchased in Macomb had been empty for 6 years. The town was growing on the opposite side of town and the city fathers were looking for opportunities to revitalize this rather overlooked side. A former supermarket made a great open space for church. With 57,000 square feet of space under roof and 300 parking places on a 6-acre corner, the facility looked pretty good. It sat on Macomb's main thoroughfare, and only a few blocks from the Western Illinois University campus. While the asking price of 1.3 million was overpriced for the location, at $750,000.00, it was a great deal.

The former Kirksville shoe factory was so large at over 100,000 square feet under roof, it severely limited potential buyers. It sat on 15 hilltop acres just south of town with an asking price of $895,000.00. After negotiation, our price was $500,000.00. Because the appraisal was over 1 million, we helped the seller recoup some of his investment by using the difference between the sales price and the appraisal to be a donation. This gave him a substantial charitable tax break.

The build outs in all three locations took a minimalist industrial approach with clear-coated concrete floors in the lobbies and hallways, carpeting and stackable seating in the auditoriums, and exposed and painted ceilings. A big emphasis was placed on color choices. This was an inexpensive way to create an edgy space. Lighting was also a priority, not the fixture but the effect it produces. It added warmth to a naturally cool space without high expense. Incorporating a coffee bar as a major component was also inviting. We built most of our fixtures ourselves. There is no doubt that they don't look as professional as the ones we've seen in high end churches. We have much more of an amateur look, but in the absence of competition, it shines and costs are minimal. We do spend money on children's areas, student areas, and in technology. We also splurge on our baptistery.

A new facility or a complete overhaul of an existing facility is a huge game-changer in a micropolitan community. It is something that people can see from the outside and it speaks volumes to them. It says that you are not satisfied with the usual. It says you are going to lay down some personal comfort in an effort to build a bridge to new people. Smaller things are big news in micropolitans. People will talk about it, be curious about it, and want to investigate. Each physical change further redefines your vision and passion to the outside world and to the church. Just take heart that is doesn't always have to be ultra-expensive.

Emphasis on Children

All of our children's areas have wonderful murals painted on the walls. When we were at Lifechurch.tv, we were blown away by their attention to the children's areas and sought to reproduce the effect here. When we investigated their sources and realized that there was no way we could afford it, we sought out our own artist. He was a friend of our children's minister and lived in South Africa. We arranged to fly him over and commissioned him to paint and do some construction. His labor was only $5,000.00, only a fraction of what Lifechurch's source would have been. We flew him over again for our Macomb location. When we started on Kirksville and contacted him, he was unwilling to come over again so quickly. We found someone else from a lead in the Kirksville group who did a wonderful job. In our early childhood areas, we installed bubble machines. It's a $100 item, but it is incredible fun for the little ones. We also made security and parental supervision a priority. Targeting the unchurched 80% means that their parents won't necessarily trust the church with their kids. Sexual misconduct has made the unchurched wary of strangers and the church environment. Our job is to put them at ease. We do this by letting parents sign in with their children if they wish. Once they're comfortable enough to leave them, we have observation areas with close circuit TV so they can monitor their children's progress while taking in the service. Once they trust us, they feel comfortable leaving them. We also take security very seriously. All children are electronically signed in. Only the guardian that signs them in can have access to pick them up. We do this with computer check in, identification tags, and numbers. With custody issues and pedophilia in our culture, security is of utmost importance. This is critically important for the outward and downward focused church.

Along with the murals and security, we installed indoor playplaces that were strategically placed in full view of the lobby. I found our first playplace on ebay. I was visiting James River Assembly and was impressed by their use of a playplace. When I checked out the cost, I put it out of my head except for a regular search on ebay. Sure enough, one in Chicago popped up. They didn't get any bids on it so I contacted them to see if they might be willing to donate it as a tax right off. I found out that they were also a church meeting in a community college and their pastor had grown up only a few miles from our church. They ended up just giving it to us. Some churches would have balked at using such key space for a playplace, but for us it was a magnet. Parents coming in with reluctant kids would find them excited by what they saw. It's presence declared what a priority children were to us. Since then, we have incorporated playplaces in all our locations. Many micropolitan areas are small enough that they don't have an indoor play area in town. The Crossing has used our playplaces to have mother's get-togethers with their children through the week. It's been one of our best investments. The maker and designer of these playplaces now attends our church and we would be happy to provide any information necessary.

An emphasis on children is another major game-changer. There is nothing more important to young families than their children. Just watch the camcorders at the next recital, the costs incurred for dance costumes, or the amount of time disposed to follow the traveling team. When the church makes kids a priority, it captures their parents. It's as simple as that.

Technology

Technology doesn't have to be near as expensive in a micropolitan church as in metropolitan areas. The entire technical package that goes into our locations is less than $150,000.00, which includes everything. While it might be inferior to megachurches, a micropolitan has never seen anything like it. While an appendix includes a list of some of the specific equipment we use, I will explain the strategy behind our technology.

Our technology fits into a space that reflects our desired target. Since we are pushing down on the dot, it will be edgy and counter-cultural for a micropolitan community. Our worship spaces are simple windowless rectangles so we can control lighting. We put the stage on the long wall to bring the crowd forward. We have steps the entire length of the stage for people to come forward and leave enough space between the stage steps and the first row of chairs to allow people to kneel at least 3 deep. We put connecting points for people to pray with others, ask questions, or receive counsel in the back corners of the auditorium. We place obstacles around outside doors to encourage people to leave through the center ones. This way they run into more conversations and ministry opportunities.

Unlike many churches, we only exhibit one style of worship. This tightens the focus on our target and our philosophy of moving people to "it's not about me". We control the lighting to the element of worship we're in. When singing, we use intelligent lighting moving to the music enhanced by hazors. House lighting is down for the music, up some for the sermon, back down for decision times, and up for announcements. Lighting control and good lighting instruments are essential for these effects. Sound is controlled from the rear of the auditorium and the stage. Configurations differ by location but it is something one feels as well as hears. Both volume and equalization are determined with our primary target in mind.

Video technology at the Crossing incorporates live feed technology to our other campuses. It would seem that cameras, projectors, screens, presentation software, computers, and live technology would be cost prohibitive. Nothing could be further from the truth. We run 4 cameras into a video switcher, choosing new shots every few seconds. We do layovers for titles, scriptures, and lyrics. We broadcast live through the internet that requires only 2 meg of continuous bandwidth. We don't have to use expensive satellite time. Our hardware is less than $7,000.00 for live video feed. Instead of getting more expensive, we continually figure out ways to do it better and cheaper at the same time. David Crowder and his band recently did a concert here using our technology exclusively and loved it.

Nothing that we are doing technology is particularly new. Large metropolitan churches are ahead of us on the curve. The differences that are important are twofold. First, we are doing this in community that has never seen it before. They have nothing local to compare it to. It may remind them of an experience they had at a major event or a previous big city church experience, but where it is makes it unique. Second, we have figured out how to do it without spending truckloads of money. Technology costs can be ridiculous. I was having a conversation with a prominent pastor from a large metropolitan church at a retreat. I had drawn a crowd after speaking about how little we paid for virtually the same product most of them had. This one pastor was unimpressed and began touting the virtues of the HD technology his church had purchased. Just one of his cameras cost more than our entire video package. I told him that the world's most well defined picture is not always beneficial, as neither of us have the prettiest face to look at. He didn't think it was funny. Sometimes a little less definition is better! In any case, the micropolitan community has no competition in this area so the technology bar can be a little lower and more money is available for necessities.

Technology is another game-changer for the micropolitan church. It sets itself apart from other churches by speaking the language of the world without compromising the message of the Lord. It opens up doors to new venues and frameworks of ministry. The Crossing has soldiers watching in Iraq and Afghanistan. We have people tuning in from almost every state. Keeping up with technology is going to be a major tipping point for the churches who continue to do ministry in the future.

Worship

From our first days as a micropolitan church, it has been our worship experience that has defined our first impression. Since we are looking to attract the 80%, we won't get many second chances so we craft our experiences with that in mind. The 80% don't like to see exorbitant amounts of money spent on aesthetics any more than church people do. Simplicity and creativity speak to them. Our buildings, lobbies, and worship areas reflect this principle. They put people at ease since they are not intimidated by their surroundings. We seek to reinforce that "come as you are" attitude with our conversation areas, coffee bars, and information kiosks. We level the field with a constant influx of new songs in worship. Most of our songs have a relatively short shelf life. The lights are down enough for newcomers to feel inconspicuous. The music is loud enough that their voice won't stand out if they choose to sing. Everything around them is contrary to their pre-conceived notion of what to expect out of a church. The stage has no permanent furniture, no pulpit, or choir loft. The performers are dressed down, giving permission to everyone to "be yourself" and be comfortable. The sermons are more "how to" than "ought to" in nature; both funny and encouraging. They are hard hitting when appropriate and non-compromising on biblical truth.

Newcomers don't know what will happen and that makes them nervous. We do our best to let them know we aren't going to embarrass them. The need for personal space is magnified in a church environment for the 80%. Recently, I attended a church where the invitation time had men standing around the stage to assist people in their decisions. If someone came forward, they escorted them to a room somewhere in the back. If I were a visitor, there would be no way I would go up there. It was far too intimidating. Where were they taking people? What were they doing to them? Later, they sought to recognize their visitors by clapping and asking them to raise their hands to receive a church brochure. There would be no way my hand would go up. This church clearly did not put themselves in the position of visitors. The worship service sets the parameters of expectation. Confrontational moments need to be carefully measured and communicated for the benefit of the 80%. The two highest confrontational points in our experiences are invitation and communion. We are clear during the invitation to tell people that if they come forward to pray, no one will bother them. This is between them and the Lord. If they wish to share it with someone, pastors stand way over on the sides and are available, not standing in the middle and looking longingly in their faces. If they have questions or want someone to pray with them, we direct them to the connecting points in the back corners of the auditorium. Communion can also be confrontational. We post instructions with the 80% in mind on our screens while we share it together. Because of our emphasis on discipleship, we do not consider the worship time to be our primary teaching time. We want to accomplish that with an intentional leader in a relational environment. We do however consider it to be our primary attractional method so we use it to connect them to small groups. We do that in the sermon, the connecting points, and the announcements. Our most predominate kiosk is small group sign-up.

There is one thing that may seem like a throwback that we splurge on...the baptistery. Our baptisteries are big enough to fit a whole family or small group in the water at the same time. They have a zero edge so water continuously flows over the edge like a quiet waterfall. It has a stone look, imitating the mikveh in Israel's history. It has become a focal point in our services. Every baptism in every service is filmed and produced into a short video. We show the previous week's baptisms at each service. Other than that, we don't give the congregation much to focus on.

I've often been asked why don't have a cross in the front of our auditorium. It's not that I have something against crosses or stained glass windows. I just don't think there is any substitute for witnessing a person change right before your eyes. Every time I share the story of the person standing next to me who is willing to let it be known, it reminds everyone there what we are all about. It's the same with the stories shared in the baptistery. I think this is where someone sees Christ most vividly. I love to see people on their knees at the steps, reaching for the Kleenex during the second worship set of our service. Our church becomes a launching pad for hope and victory. This image reminds us all that the facility or the technology will always take a back seat to what is truly important.

Worship is the most infamous game-changer in today's church. It has opened a virtual Pandora's box of issues and arguments. Every week we get feedback telling us to turn it down, to sing more familiar songs, to target a wider audience, to use less technology and so forth. I have to continually remind the church and myself that we have a "bigger yes". It's a bigger yes that's paid off in people. The Crossing isn't the 27th fastest growing church in America because it's trying to be like other churches. It's working because we have made the lost children of God our biggest priority. We push that dot down every day keeping our eyes outward and trust in Jesus to meet our need from His boundless supply. Our unapologetic approach to worship fits this strategy.

Music is a big part of most of our lives. We all have expensive radios in our cars to fit our musical needs. XM and Sirius radio gives us more options. iPods keep our favorite music at our constant disposal. iTunes has become our new record store. Music moves us emotionally connecting, us to deep places within ourselves. Musical taste is one of the most subjective areas of our lives. Some churches provide different worship experiences designed around different musical tastes. I don't necessarily think that approach is wrong but I do think it is a bit schizophrenic. We just never wanted to be a church with multiple personalities. It makes us better at doing the one approach, but sacrifices the attempt at better connecting with personal taste. Since we do teach that personal taste is something that is offered on the alter of the mature in Christ, a single approach serves us better. However, it is probably the most powerful negative for people who walk right back out the front door. Make no mistake, the price of single mindedness is very high and needs to be measured in each environment.

Teaching

Established churches in micropolitan communities probably use Sunday School classes as the primary means of Bible teaching and Christian education. Sunday School has organizational advantages over small groups that meet in homes. Most existing churches have a great deal of their facility dedicated to Sunday School so space needs are met. There are huge amounts of resources available for teaching and most churches have an organizational structure for Sunday School. It is easy to work in a built-in time at the church where childcare is available for adults and teachers are already there for kids. Churches that have multiple services either run the Sunday School simultaneously to worship or between them. Churches with a single service run Sunday School either before or after worship. This means that people are killing two birds with one stone so to speak. It means one trip, one time slot, and Sunday morning is usually free of conflicts. Simply put, Sunday School is convenient.

I wonder how many people can, like me, trace key moments in their spiritual life happening through a Sunday School class. However, it is also true that Sunday School as a program has experienced sharp declines in many churches over the past few decades. Once again, the inertia of a once-successful idea may end up using up huge amounts of precious resources of time, money, and energy without accomplishing the desired goal. The frustration of having great teaching but declining numbers is something many pastors have experienced. It also may ignore the changes in culture and how those changes apply to how people learn.

The fact that there has been spiritual impact felt through Sunday School does not validate it exclusively as the right means for Christian education and discipleship. Sunday School was originally developed in England and then America as a means of encouraging more civilized behavior from child labor in factories. Over the next 200+ years, it morphed into more of what we experience today, both for children and adults. A tough question to ask is whether or not Sunday School is the best way to teach and disciple. Tougher still is figuring out what would happen if we tried a different approach to learning. Since classroom space is equated with Christian education, it will have a big impact on approaching new construction. It might be a good exercise to calculate the percentage of square footage used for classes as compared to other spaces. Classroom spaces struggle to have good multi-use abilities.

As I shared before, the Crossing found itself in a difficult circumstance with its new building. We had incorporated a lot of space for Sunday School when we found out that it was going to be unaffordable as it was designed. Our solution was to reduce costs by prioritizing which spaces we had to have and those we wanted to have. This became our first step in a very big game-changer. We chose to replace adult Sunday School with small groups. I like to brag a bit about how easily the Crossing embraces change. This was definitely an exception to that. Many adult Sunday School classes are generational in nature. They have names and identities. People may stay with a single Sunday School class their entire adult life. Eventually the oldest class just graduates into eternity. People new to church join the class that have the people in it closest to their age. Classes have activities, take offerings, and maybe support their own mission.

When we began discussing a new building without dedicating new space for adult classes, resistance was felt. Many of these classes had people in them for years. They had received teaching from the same leader for much of that time. I call them leaders because I think we often misunderstand a person's gifting. We might want to call them teachers but I learned that their primary desire was more to be followed than to teach. Don't get me wrong…I don't think that is necessarily bad, just misunderstood. These classes were their own personal place of control and oftentimes, independence. They were used to the routine and convenience of it. The rooms had sacred objects that had been donated or made. It was a tough battle and some feelings were hurt.

Any "old dog" needs to have at least one question seriously pondered. Is this a hill I am willing to die on? People are always more important than programs and that includes both the Sunday school and the small group approach. The small group idea that we had at the time really wasn't that much better than our Sunday School. We just couldn't accommodate the space necessary to keep the status quo. However, the small group emphasis on discipleship we have today is so far superior to our past, there is really no comparison. Those ideas would have never come to us without the movement away from our conventional approach. The concepts that we incorporate into small groups today could easily be incorporated into a Sunday School structure, but it wouldn't be sustainable without lots of building space. Sunday Schools already are relational environments. They would still require an intentional leader who is focused on moving people through the reproducible process from A to D. In that process, more and more groups and leaders would be forming but classroom space would be limited. While a Sunday School would have the convenience of time, space, and child care, small groups have the advantage of meeting anytime and almost any place, without burning up a lot of church dollars or space.

Today, the Crossing is redefining leadership through reproduction. Someone who wants to lead isn't thinking about how many people he can get to follow him. Instead, he is investing in regular people moving through the reproducible process and helping would-be leaders who move on to lead themselves. Those especially gifted and committed end up in a coach's role, leading and encouraging groups of leaders. We want to resist anything that limits the overall effectiveness of that reproduction.

Organic Structure

John Maxwell writes in his leadership books about "lifting lids". This is a term he uses in regards to obstacles for growth and effectiveness. The micropolitan church will continually become a victim to its own ineffectiveness. As it grows, it will find itself in a structure that is no longer sufficient to maximize its own potential. Unless the structure changes, the church will level out underneath the lid of its self-imposed limitation. Because of this inherent danger to continued growth, organizational structure is a big game changer.

I believe the micropolitan church is much more an organism than it is an organization. Organisms are organic. What does that mean? They live! Life involves the miraculous… the supernatural. No one can artificially *produce* life as it can only be *reproduced*. It was God that brought life, a part of Himself, into the world. When something is alive, it means that it is going through a process of taking something in, transforming a portion of it into energy, and producing waste. Growth takes place. Change is always happening. Anything alive is in constant danger of death. Death is ultimately inevitable. Reproduction continues the species…and on it goes. I see the church this way. A seed is planted into the ground. The life of the plant begins in the death of the seed. Its decomposition produces germination. Before long, a small shoot breaks through the soil reaching for the light. At the same time, roots drive into the soil below, looking for water and minerals. The shoot spreads out, collecting the energy of the sun using photosynthesis. Before long, it is a full sized plant producing seed exponentially. As one plant falls and begins to decompose, it provides the soil with the nutrients and minerals the next plant will need.

Jesus said that the nature of the church is organic. He said,

> *"I tell you the truth, unless a kernel of wheat falls to the ground and dies, it remains only a single seed. But if it dies, it produces many seeds. The man who loves his life will lose it, while the man who hates his life in this world will keep it for eternal life." John 12:24-25*

So what does it mean for the church to be organic? It means that new things should be happening all the time. It means that old things are passing away all the time. It means

125

Jerry Harris

that outside of the fact that Jesus is the same and the Bible is true, the only true constant is change. It means that things are not completely predictable or controllable, that organizational structures and goals become quickly irrelevant as life happens. Isaiah says,

> *"Forget the former things, do not dwell on the past.*
> *See, I am doing a new thing! Now it springs up, do*
> *you not perceive it? I am making a way in the desert*
> *and streams in the wasteland." Isaiah 43:18-19*

The micropolitan church has to learn that the nature of the church is organic. It can't get caught up in organizational structures and policies. It can't be limited to the shortsightedness of long range planning. How can we make long range plans when the church is constantly changing and growing? The micropolitan church develops the agility to change its approach along with the circumstances around it. Resistance to change is one of the main things that prematurely kills the church. We get caught up in a particular program or approach when it was only a means to an end. Instead of figuring out new ways to achieve real growth for the Kingdom, we use all our energy propping up the ineffective until there is no life left. How many churches today are the most relevant to people long since dead and buried?

The Crossing doesn't make long-range plans. It is also careful about getting seriously married to specific plans in the short range. We like to stay in a place where the Holy Spirit can change our mind and direction at will. When the Crossing was a small church with less than 300 people I knew everybody and was involved in every ministry. I could work the sound system, lock the building, find the files I need, fill in for leading youth group, and sing a special for worship. As the church grew, I had to rely on the harvest of new workers to accomplish those things for me. Some churches don't grow

126

because pastors think that no one can do things as well as they can. Beneath that feeling is a deep-seated insecurity that if I let go, I won't be needed anymore. We find our worth in those responsibilities instead of letting God show us new things as we give up the old ones to others.

The same thing works in our organization. You could look back on the last eleven years at the Crossing and see a completely different structure each year. Each time something new is introduced, you adjust. It happens on a large scale and a small one. Organizational change has to happen around growth. The church of 300 will operate completely different than one of 700. Music, children's ministry, facility, parking, ministries, publications, employment needs, accounting, be prepared for everything to change. The organization should be built around the organism with form following function. The micropolitan church embraces this change as normal, carefully guarding against any structure to become so entrenched that it might threaten the church's health and growth.

Take a moment and think about the organic nature of our spiritual lives. We come to accept Jesus Christ as a result of belief. When Jesus spoke about belief, He always used the word "in" with it. He never said, "Believe Me.", but said, "Believe in Me.". That little word describes a fixed position. In context, it means I am placing my life in Him. When I believe in Jesus, I'm doing something more than just accepting a certain set of facts. I am standing in a new place. But how do I get there? If belief is a fixed position, repentance is my movement to that new fixed position. Repentance is "how" I believe. It is the means by which I move to a new fixed position. The sorrow I feel is not from moving to a new place, but recognizing the time I wasted at the old one. Now here is the organic part. Once I get to this new fixed position of belief through repentance, God is able to show me all sorts of new things about Himself to believe in from this new fixed position. My desire to move closer to Him results in repentance again, or the movement to another fixed position. So my Christian life is a series of steps brought on by repenting and believing and repenting and believing. As I move, I change. As I change, I move...all the while getting closer to Him as He directs me.

Now why shouldn't the church operate the same way? There are so many things the church can't see from this fixed position, so we need to give up control from too much goal setting and organizational flowcharting and just let Him lead.

Part 5: Multi-site & Micropolitan

Three fourths of this book is about becoming a micropolitan church. Using multi-site strategy is another thing altogether. Using multi-site in a micropolitan setting carries unique benefits and challenges that are substantially different than what has been previously discussed considering only one location. The following concepts may sound a bit repetitive in a few areas, but there are specifics that must be carefully focused on with multi-site strategy in mind. For instance, while you may read about attributes in the section discussing a campus pastor that sounds similar to leadership that have been discussed, they take on a completely new flavor when a multi-site campus pastor is sitting in the second chair behind a senior pastor who is the primary preacher. I would not recommend multi-site approach in a micropolitan church unless the primary location is strong enough to have enough margin to sustain the risk. However, carefully implemented, it can bring impact for the Kingdom previously thought impossible. It is here to stay. A bigger question for micropolitan communities is how the strategy can be used effectively to spread the gospel and build the kingdom in a small town setting. The following insights from an article in the Christian Standard helps us all to see that multi-site is more than just the latest flavor.

Latest Flavor or Lasting Paradigm?

About 20 years ago, Dave Ferguson used a restaurant's napkin to scribble his dream for one church meeting in multiple locations, starting in Chicago and reproducing everywhere. A little more than a decade ago, North Coast Church launched its first satellite site near its San Diego facility. Across the country a couple of years later, Seacoast Church went multi-site around Charleston, South Carolina. Just over six years ago, a Leadership Journal article penned by Ferguson opened with a prediction: "The multi-site church is a phenomenon that you will no doubt be hearing about in the future." Three years ago a seminal book entitled *The Multi-Site Church Revolution* (Zondervan; 2006) forecast that "50 years from now, we believe multi-venue and multi-site will be the norm." But by the spring of 2008, multi-site already was being dubbed "the new normal" by Willow magazine (which serves congregations associated with Willow Creek Community Church in suburban Chicago). Now SeaCoast is gathering at 13 locations in three states with an average weekend attendance of 10,000, up from 3000 when it met in one location. It has been named one of the 15 most influential churches in the United States. North Coast has about 7000 coming to either four remote sites or a dozen venues at the main campus; nearly triple the amount from the days before multi-site. Since Community Christian went multi-site in 1998, attendance zoomed from 800 to more than 5000 spread over 9 locations.

One thing's for sure: the trend line is impressive. Statistics compiled by Community Christian show the number of multi-site churches has rocketed from 10 in 1990 to 100 in 1998 to 1500 in 2004. Currently one out of four megachurches has gone multi-site, and a third of all churches are considering it. Seven of America's 10 fastest-growing churches are multi-site, and nine of the 10 largest churches are multi-site. Geoff Surratt, lead author of the Multi-Site Church Revolution and ministries pastor at Seacoast said Willow's characterization of multi-site churches as "the new normal" is a bit of hyperbole. "The revolution, however, is gaining momentum," he said. "There are very few towns of any size in America without at least one multi-site church. Many smaller churches are exploring the idea of connecting with a larger church in a direct partnership. I think we are just beginning to see the potential of this form of church."

Chris Mavity, who has conducted multi-site seminars for leaders from more than 1000 churches as executive director of the North Coast Training Network said at first the sessions centered on whether the concept would work. "That question's already been answered now," he said. "It's really not a question of will it work, but whether this is a direction we should take." North Coast actually is more of a multi-venue church than a multi-site. Attendees at the Evangelical Free Church have a choice of four other campuses, but those going to the main facility at an old warehouse complex in Vista, California have their pick of at least a dozen styles of worship. Like many multi-site churches, the new venture was born of desperation: North Coast was simply out of space. "The idea was to crate an overflow room," Mavity said. But North Coast leaders also realized that overflow rooms often are "the dungeon of the church," so they strived to make the new venue "an alternative worship experience." Thus was born the video café', led by Mavity, just off the church plaza where attendees heard live contemporary music, then watched the message on a large video screen as they sipped Starbucks coffee and sampled pastries. "It was an immediate success," Mavity said. The new venue attracted 173 the first Sunday and averaged 493 after a year, 1200 after two years, and 2200 after 3. "It wasn't because we were great, it wasn't because we're more spiritual than other churches, it was because the opportunity was there. And what we didn't know was that the culture was ready for the video experience."

Now those attending North Coast have their choice of such venues as country/gospel (feel free to wear your cowboy hat and sit on the hay bales); Traditions, a softer ambience featuring a blend of traditional and contemporary hymns; the Message, with its coffeehouse atmosphere; Frontline, an acoustic worship catering to military personnel; and the Edge, with urban art and subwoofer-backed worship that is a wee bit louder than the others. These gatherings meet anytime from 5:40 pm Saturday to 6:30 pm Sunday. And all except three North Coast Live services get the sermon (usually from senior pastor Larry Osborne) via video screen. "We found a way through these venues to actually get healthier as a church because we are providing worship styles that are preferred rather than put up with," said Mavity. Explaining the church's growth to 7000, "There'd be no way we'd have that many people with just one worship style." And he adds two statements likely to resonate with church leaders nationwide: "It's a lot cheaper to start a venue than build a building. We just don't have worship wars anymore."

Surratt says a church cannot pull off multi-site without quality, especially in the video presentation. Three fourths of those who attend SeaCoast see the messages from his brother, senior pastor Greg Surratt, on a video screen. "You don't need Broadway, but you do need better than a junior high sock hop," he said. "If Ruth's Chris Steakhouse's second location had opened with a menu of mystery meat and mac and cheese, there would never have been a third location." And he cautions that multi-site won't work on its own.

He bristles a bit when asked whether multi-site simply caters to America's consumerist, "it's—all-about-me" society. "I think that is a valid criticism of most churches in America," Surratt said. "We install electricity, air conditioning, and indoor plumbing simply to cater to the whims of society. While I am being somewhat facetious, it is easy to point at other churches for being consumer minded while ignoring how much in your church is really the same." He also says the multi-site church is as scriptural as other models. "I think in the Acts churches you can see elements of multi-site churches, megachurches, and small parish churches. I do not see anything in Scripture that prevents multi-site as a method, nor do I see anything that endorses multi-site as 'more biblical' than other models."

He predicts the multi-site movement will soon branch in several directions at once. In the new book, *A Multi-site Church Roadtrip* (Zondervan 2009); like his previous book, written with Greg Ligon and Warren Bird), 15 innovations impacting multi-site churches across the country are examined. "We are seeing trends such as internet campuses, international campuses, and campuses launching campuses as churches are finding more and more creative ways to reach people with the good news," Surratt said. Meanwhile, Ferguson, the senior pastor at Community Christian, now calls his vision scrawled onto that napkin nearly two decades ago a dream from God. After opening its second site, Community Christian more than quadrupled in size, mostly with previously unchurched people. Another seven locations, including one Spanish speaking service, have been added in the past eight years, with more to come.

Yet multi-site is more about quality than quantity, Ferguson says. "It's about taking who you are, reproducing the ethos or quality experience of your church, and bringing it to more people," he wrote in Outreach magazine a couple of years ago. "Once you have established that quality, why not reproduce it? Why start from scratch?" Community Christian has discovered that the retention rate is higher for the multi-site locations; 58 to 65 percent of those who attended the first service came back, compared to its original church plant. Ferguson envisions multi-site churches becoming more influential than megachurches in the near future, and leads a network of new and reproducing churches called New Thing. Dramatic is the word for the church's ultimate vision for the Chicago area: 200 sites attended by 100,000 people every week.**10**

None of the examples used in the article occur in micropolitan settings. Books already written about multi-site (I know of three) find their examples in metropolitan settings, leading us to believe multi-site has been pretty much an exclusively metropolitan phenomenon...or so I thought...

The Perfect Marriage: Multi-site and Micropolitan

It won't work! Not in the Midwest! I could see it happening in Chicago or Los Angeles, but not in the heartland of America, especially small communities like ours. Who would want to look at a preacher on a screen instead of live? Couldn't you just stay home and watch church on TV? I disregarded the concept of video venues before the term "multi-site" was being used to describe a new way of launching churches. Geoff Surratt met a similar attitude when SeaCoast Church first began experimenting with the multi-site concept, "When SeaCoast started our first campus, everyone thought we were crazy. I seemed to have an endless line at my office door of staff saying this will never work, and other churches told us again and again that video teaching was dumb idea." Seven years and 7000 new attendees later it seems like everyone wants to open multiple campuses.**11**

The Crossing had been experiencing a great deal of growth and space was a constant concern. The stopgap measures we had taken on the way to a new auditorium reaped some unexpected benefits. One critical concept I personally learned came when we were forced to use cameras and image magnification. We had completely run out of space in our auditorium and couldn't figure out a way to add another service. It was crazy the way it was. We had seven minutes between services to move people out and in. The worship team just continued playing without a break. We decided to break out the back wall of the stage and use the space behind it to place an additional 200 chairs. That meant that there were people in front of me and behind me while preaching. To keep the ones behind me only having the view of my backside, we introduced cameras and image magnification so that they could see the forward image. Two things happened. First, it taught me how to preach with a camera. Second, and most important, it taught me that people are actually very comfortable with looking at the screen instead of me. I remember looking directly at people in the first few rows trying to make eye contact, but they were looking away from me to the screen. It actually made sense. You could see facial expressions and follow the sermon better. Chris Mavity from North Coast Church adds, "That was something the entertainment industry had discovered years before; unless people are in the first few rows of a live event, they often watch the game or the concert on a large video screen simply because they can see better. The same is true at most large churches where the speaker or worship leader is shown on a video screen."12

The lack of space and the use of image magnification started to open my heart up to more innovative approaches to get the vision of an intimate personal relationship with Christ out in ways we hadn't thought of before. Earlier in this book, I shared how we came in contact with Lifechurch.tv and saw an incredibly effective multi-site model in Oklahoma City and several other cities. At this writing, Lifechurch.tv is the second largest church of any kind in the country. As of 2009, they average almost 27,000 in attendance in all their locations and remain the 13th fastest growing church, nearly 4 times the size they were in 2005 when we went to check them out. However, the multi-site strategy is almost exclusively a metropolitan phenomenon. Trying it in a micropolitan community is a completely different animal.

While it was true that the Crossing had been growing at an awesome rate in Quincy, in the back of my mind I felt there might be a time when we had so saturated the community, that most everyone who was going to try us out already had. That would never even be a thought in a metropolitan city. That is just a part of the contrast between metro and micro cultures. While the Crossing became a big fish relatively quickly, it accomplished it in a small pond. As discussed before, there just weren't any other marketable alternatives, giving the Crossing a virtual monopoly on innovation and relevance. In the metro culture, the body of water is more like a lake than a pond. There are many more people to pull from but also the competition of potentially many innovative church options. People can view church options like restaurants, pushing the consumer mentality to much deeper levels.

Just the thought of finding an end to the explosive growth we had experienced, and the opportunities it had brought to drive people deeper into discipleship pushed me into the unusual and risky idea of multi-site. It was going to require a major shift in virtually every organizational structure and ministry. Not only that, the congregation was going to have to buy into something very uncomfortable, outside the norm. Our leaders had never thought in these terms before either.

I call multi-site a quantum leap for a reason, especially in a micropolitan setting. Being self-serving is human nature. We have already discussed how difficult it is for many churches to truly become outwardly focused. It is just easier to sing the songs we already know, to worship in a space that we're used to, and to stand next to the same people we stood with last week. But going multi-site is a leap the likes of which the church has never seen. We can get motivated to work with youth, give to a new building project, or to hire a new ministry position, but when we start exporting lots of money and energy to a community that we don't even live in or know people, that is another thing. Many multi-site churches exist in metropolitan areas where people have to drive an extra 15 or 20 minutes to get to church. They exist where the "mother church" lets a few hundred church members start in a new location. They have a built in financial base, a core of people, and proximity to the parent campus.

The micropolitan church going multi-site is a quantum leap because it goes into a community too far away to shift a core of people from the parent church. Without that core, the new work loses a guaranteed amount of money and the security of proximity. It is being outwardly focused on another level like swinging on the trapeze without a net beneath you. In a sense, it is "enhanced" church planting. The challenge is to help the leadership to see not only the need for a church in another area, but be willing to put the resources behind it in a substantial level. This requires a high level of commitment and risk to the forward movement of the gospel, even if we never personally receive any expected benefit from it.

Biblical Example: Men from Cyprus and Cyrene

There is an often overlooked verse in Acts 11 that captured my heart as I began to think about the prospects of going multi-site in a micropolitan way.

*"Now those who had been scattered by the persecution
in connection with Stephen traveled as far as Phoenicia,
Cyprus and Antioch, telling the message only to Jews.
Some of them, however, men from Cyprus and Cyrene,
went to Antioch and began to speak to Greeks also,
telling them the good news about the Lord Jesus.
The Lord's hand was with them, and a great number of people
believed and turned to the Lord."*

I think we find it easy to read over this passage of scripture without realizing the weight of it. These men with no recorded names from Cyprus and Cyrene are some of my biggest heroes of the New Testament, serving as our multi-site example. Go back to the maps section in the back of your Bible and just look at how far Cyprus and Cyrene are from Antioch. Cyprus over 100 miles away from Antioch and Cyrene was over a whopping 1000 miles away! What would cause these men to walk away from the familiar and their families to go to a foreign country to start a church? Weren't there needs on the Island of Cyprus? Didn't North Africa need the gospel as well? What would cause them to reach across culture, language, and religion, to establish this new work?

We usually call the trip that Paul and Barnabas took in Acts 13 the first missionary journey. I would submit that such a journey might never have happened if it weren't for these nameless men. The church they established broke through the barrier of Judaism before Paul's efforts and became the new capital of Christianity after the destruction of Jerusalem. Antioch was where Barnabas brought Paul to cut his teeth in ministry. Paul was there for a year playing a supporting role to the work of the men from Cyprus and Cyrene. I'm sure much of Paul's DNA for reaching outside the Jewish culture and going out into the world was shaped by the work of these special men. It was where we first wore the name "Christian" and was the base from which Paul launched out to reach the whole known world for Christ. It was truly a missional church, born out the simple desire of these men from Cyprus and Cyrene. There was something of them in every victory that followed and every new church that was established. I believe that like them, when we are moved to do something that is truly selfless, the Lord's hand will be with us. If we can embrace the humility of the nameless, God will accomplish the most and receive the greatest glory.

8 Multi-site Hurdles

When the Crossing went to Macomb, we were expanding our strategy from Acts 2 to Acts 11, trying to catch the same fresh wind that filled the sails of these men so long ago. We had no template to build from, no model that we could identify with outside of what we had seen in Oklahoma City at Lifechurch.tv. Although there were some multi-site strategies out there, we weren't aware of them, and the kind of micropolitan setting we were looking to work in hadn't been done before. Below are some steps that we have we have gone through in the implementation of coupling micropolitan and multi-site strategies. As our stories will confirm, these steps never came in a neat order. They are only arranged this way because it seems logical, but remember, since the church is more organism than organization, flexibility is key as the Holy Spirit directs the process.

1st Hurdle: Choose a micropolitan

The Crossing's Multi-site Micropolitans

Our choice of a community to start our first multi-site came fairly quickly. We realized that we were going to have to have our hands all over this first experience, so we had to be close enough to be able to send work crews and staff to help get things going. We also needed to be far enough that those who would attend, wouldn't otherwise come to the Crossing. We drew a circle that showed a 60-mile radius around Quincy on a map to see what micropolitans were available. Process of elimination brought Macomb to the forefront. We had no desire to go to a micropolitan that already had a progressive church like ours. Unfortunately, there weren't any of those in a 60-mile radius so that didn't narrow it much. With a population of 20,000 and a student body of 13,000, Macomb had plenty of evangelistic opportunity. It didn't have any churches that had an attendance of over 300. We liked the idea that Macomb was the home of Western Illinois University. We felt that a university atmosphere would promote a willingness to embrace new things. Being somewhat economically depressed, it provided some less expensive purchasing opportunities. Macomb also had a reputation of being a spiritually dark place and we were drawn to the challenge of that.

The choice of Kirksville came from the launch of Macomb. A few families from Kirkville heard what we were doing and came to check us out. They attended the launch of Macomb and made a pitch to our leaders to see if we might consider doing it again in Kirksville. Although a somewhat smaller micropolitan, Kirksville still had a population of 17,000 and an additional 6,000 at Truman State University. It also had no church of any size or a progressive approach. Unlike the new highway to Macomb, Kirksville also had the challenge of a 90-minute drive on a two-lane road to get there. There was also the consideration of being across state lines and the ramifications that might have, especially with live technology.

We are presently investigating a leasing option in Burlington, Iowa. It is a convention center attached to a theme park and a casino…definitely a gamble! Burlington has a population of about 30,000 and like our other sites, has no other progressive church option. We are excited about another prospect on the horizon and as we draw circles around each location, it becomes clearer that the Crossing now has become a regional church. We have locations in many of the major micropolitan communities all around us and small groups in most of the small towns between them.

Our South Africa site came as a result of the desire of our Quincy campus children's pastor, Barry Stander. A native Afrikaner, he had come to America with his wife and two children on a visa to work with us. After 3 incredible years, he had to make a decision whether to naturalize or return. He had always had a heart for church planting and he loved the paradigm of the Crossing. He approached the leadership with the idea of establishing a location in Mosselbay, a micropolitan town of 40,000 on the coastal Garden Road between Port Elizabeth and Capetown. Once again, there was no other church like us anywhere near, and no church of any size in town. It had access to many townships and didn't have an integrated church in the community.

Your Multi-site Micropolitan

It's exciting to dream regionally, even internationally, instead of just locally. I encourage you to make a map of your area with a 120-mile radius and look at the communities represented there. There might be some that you will want to eliminate because there is already great ministry happening there, but if they are micropolitans, they probably don't. Which ones are the closest but still outside of your local influence? What potential resources do you have in those areas? What does the religious footprint look like? How spiritually dark is the area? Just think of the potential impact a micropolitan church could have for the families and individuals there! Your church could be the difference that changes the face of a community and the lives of those who live there!

When choosing a community to work in, start by asking yourself what kind of impact for the kingdom you think is there. Micropolitans don't need churches with similar approaches competing with each other for members. If it's your first site, consider the fact that you will need to be close enough to be hands on. We considered Macomb our great experiment. It's success was crucial to our leaders and congregation if we were going to cast a vision to go anywhere else. Your choice might be a more obvious one because it's clear that the Lord is leading in that direction. It could come from an obvious leader that is established in the area. It could come from facility that comes available. It could come from a core group that rises up wanting to make a difference in their micropolitan community that buys into the vision and approach of your church. It's obvious that the Crossing didn't and doesn't have a canned way of selecting communities, as it has been a highly organic process.

Additional Extension Sites Within One Micropolitan

An extension campus is designed around a specific need of ministry in a micropolitan community with an already existing micropolitan church. If you have a specific need that your congregation is spiritually tuned to, an extension campus might be a great option. The costs will be a fraction of what a full-service campus would be. The benefits to both the original campus and the targeting group could be amazing. It might be based on ministry that is age targeted if your church has opportunities for the elderly or college/career age. It might be culture or language targeted to Hispanics or Asians. Like ours, it might be more economically targeted. In any case, an extension campus builds a bridge to accomplish the vision and create fellowship with specific groups otherwise kept apart because of these barriers.

Our fifth campus was launched out of our desire to connect with people that would come to us out of primarily benevolent need. Although Quincy is a small enough town to only need one Crossing, we saw an opportunity to reach out to a population group that we were only marginally hitting. We found an old church building in the inner city of Quincy with the potential of reaching a subset of our population that had been difficult to connect with for economic, cultural, and transportation reasons. The cost of the building was extremely low. We were able to fund the purchase of the campus and procure all the money to bring it up to standards with a single offering on a single Sunday.

2ⁿᵈ *Hurdle: Choose a Campus Pastor*

Multi-site is now the latest fad in church growth, but it is failed strategy if there is not a compelling vision behind it. "That means getting the proper people to head the effort. The biggest challenge is finding the right leaders for campus pastors." Geoff Surratt says. "Churches who select strong entrepreneurial leaders tend to see a great deal of growth at their offsite campuses; churches who simply choose managers or administrators tend to struggle. Multi-site is not a shortcut to recruiting, mentoring, and releasing strong leaders."[13] I have to say that this step and the person selected is the most critical component to the success of the multi-site strategy. The campus pastor has to lead from the second chair. He communicates the senior pastor's vision while being its main cheerleader on the campus where he's planted. Campus pastors need to be great leaders with enough skill to manage all the needs of a new group of mostly strangers, recognizing their gifts and giving them ministry opportunity. He is responsible for managing a new staff, keeping a unified attitude to the overall vision, counseling, establishing and managing small groups, and working toward campus viability. New campuses will rely heavily on their campus pastor creating a great deal of stress for his position. Simply put, the campus pastor is a human picture of the campus itself. The success or failure of the campus and the pastor are tied together.

The first and most critical requirement of the campus pastor is that he possesses the same DNA as the church he represents. He absolutely cannot have a different vision as his position is the critical link that binds the multi-site campus to the church as a whole. At the Crossing, we do not believe that we can hire this person externally. There is just no way to instill that DNA to an outsider. If we did hire someone externally, they would be working in a ministerial role inside the church for enough time for our leadership team to be convinced that they would die on a hill for our approach before they would ever be considered for such a critical role. Let me illustrate this with two stories; one of success and one of failure.

While we were in the planning process for our Macomb multi-site campus, we began to watch and pray for the person that would be the right leader. We were already using interns in some of our ministries. Two guys were traveling 6 hours one-way each weekend to work in our youth ministries, one primarily in teaching and the other in worship. After their graduation from Bible College, they continued on with us in full time roles. Clayton was the first intern to graduate and began teaching and ministering full time as an associate at the Quincy campus. Ben continued his internship and was hired as the new campus was preparing to launch. We knew that Clayton had incredible potential as a leader, but was young and single with little experience. However, the demographic of our target in Macomb matched him perfectly. The median age of the town was 23, greatly reduced because of the presence of the university. About a year before the launch, we decided to give him the offer. Clayton has admitted that at first, his thought had been, "I wonder who the chump is going to be that will take that job?" He saw it as a meaningless 2nd fiddle role. When the offer came to him, he had mixed emotions.

Because of his initial feelings, he had to think about what it was going to be like living in Macomb and giving up some ideas and dreams about being a lead pastor at his own independent church. Looking back, Clayton would tell you that his decision to become the lead pastor in Macomb has been one of the greatest of his life. Ben came on as their worship pastor after his graduation. Two years later, the Crossing Macomb is a passionate, growing congregation consisting of mostly new believers excited about their new relationship with Jesus and living it out in daily life. Clayton has been challenged to the extreme but has zealously protected the connection he has with the rest of the campuses. The church now meets its own financial needs and is a true partner in ministry. They are presently raising up internal leadership and aggressively pursuing their discipleship strategy. How many 26 year olds have the opportunity to be in charge of a church of 1000 people with a 56,000 square foot campus? Being connected to the rest of us is like working with a net. Things that would have taken years to accomplished have been reduced to weeks and months because of our connection. Clayton's effective ministry life span has also greatly increased. The fact that he has exactly the same DNA has been the critical piece in the campus's success.

A Big Mistake and God's Faithfulness

I consider the role of campus pastor as the critical link in the multi-site micropolitan model as much out of reaction by past experience as anything else. The lessons I learned from doing it wrong have been a great benefit as the Crossing has failed forward. Our vulnerability came from an unlikely place... success. As we watched and participated in the incredible success of Macomb, we developed arrogance that our multi-site model was bulletproof. We began to have a "just add water" mentality, thinking that failure was impossible because of the inherent positives of being micropolitan. We thought, "No big deal! Let's do it again!" when approached by the core group from Kirksville. While we did most of our homework right, we made a defining mistake when looking for a campus pastor. There was no one being raised up from the Quincy campus at the time. We later found our flaws described in Jim Collin's great little book, *How the Mighty Fall*. The first flaw was a hard one to see in the church. Jim calls it ***the insatiable pursuit of more***. The desire to grow the Kingdom of God and bring people into an intimate personal relationship with Christ could hardly be considered a flaw. Yet without the right attitude that generates the best questions to ask internally, the pursuit of more can move us down paths outside of God's leading. We looked at the families who were regularly driving 90 minutes one-way for over a year and their desire to be a core for a new work in Kirksville, a kind of Macedonian Call. The biggest problem with the pursuit of more in our case was how quickly it led us to our second flaw, ***hubris born out of success***.

Truman State University had an active campus ministry. The director of that ministry contacted us wanting to know our church planting plans. A short time after meeting with him, he contacted us about his desire to lead the new campus. He was well loved and connected in the area, had twenty-five years of ministry experience, and had a stated desire to be part of our team. I saw it as God meeting our need, heavily relying on my belief that our model was so great, that nothing could diminish its effectiveness. Because of my arrogance, I pushed the hire forward without properly understanding the critical nature of our DNA. There was really very little done as for the training process. Before long, he was on staff and making recommendations on other local staff hiring. Of the other four positions, we allowed him to push two forward. Before we ever launched, we could easily see serious issues in all sorts of areas that didn't match up to us in work ethic, management, passion, unity, staff polarization, and gifting. We made an attempt to repair the situation by moving his role to something more fitting to what we perceived as his gifting. Our attempts failed us and an infant church family was forced to endure the resignation of three of its five staff and the loss of about 100 people.

It was in the midst of this train wreck that we realized one of the greatest positive inherent components of the multi-site system. Because all of our campuses reflect a single church, we were able to compensate for the staff loss by positioning present staff temporarily to Kirksville. I went to Kirksville to preach and explain our situation and our elders took a more visual role. The campuses were able to compensate the heavy financial losses that came from reduced giving. What could have been a mortal wound eventually amounted more as a loss of momentum and a reinstitution of the Crossing's core values into the Kirksville campus. The attendance losses were recovered within 4 months and staff replacements aided in spiritual health. We moved the former youth minister into the campus pastor role. It was amazing to see just how much safety and security exists in a cord of three strands not easily being broken.

As I reflect on what I've learned from the experience and the mistakes, I think that I, like many visionary leaders, are natural optimists. We tend to want to look at everyone through the rose-colored glasses of what their potential is. While that may sound great on the surface, it can also lead to some debilitating circumstances if fueled by a dismissiveness brought on by arrogance. It's the same unrealistic attitude that allows pastors to be hired into churches that are bad fits. Like a bad marriage, we think that by sheer force of will, we can change the nature of a church or a staff member. One megachurch founding pastor on the west coast considered his unrealistic and overly optimistic view of those around him to be his greatest professional flaw. It certainly can get us into some very painful and messy situations. If we couple that optimism with a successful model, it can make it easy to cut corners in a process designed to produce a great result and protect a great idea.

I believe all campus pastor hires have to be internal. That doesn't mean that they don't have professional training, it just means that they need to have been in the church at some level for a reasonable amount of time. There is just no way to teach our core values, our DNA, in a short period of time or to expect that through a series of interviews or a relationship outside of the church, a good fit is guaranteed. This decision above all others keeps the multi-site concept a well-working part of one church working together in harmony and unity. The campus pastor is the local face of the church as a whole so his personality weighs heavily on the decision.

These 5 questions encapsulate the main areas of required effectiveness that we look for in a campus pastor.

1. Can he be a leader and still give up his personal will for a greater good?

A campus pastor must be the one who casts the vision of the church to his people, but realizing that it is a shared vision and not exclusively his. This is a place where pride and personal agenda can get in the way. He has to be able to effect change, set attainable goals, and be innovative with ideas that make the vision work in his local setting. He will be required to make quick and effective decisions, equip and empower leaders under his authority, and maintain a comprehensive evaluation process. Someone with these skills might be more inclined to pursue a ministry without so much interconnectivity. Recognizing the benefit of a larger, more regional church and working in a more participating rather than primary role in its leadership is a big step. It's the difference between pastor and campus pastor.

2. Can he be a pastor to his people?

There are certain responsibilities that are just considered the nuts and bolts of ministry that are all underneath the heading of pastor. These would include counseling, marriages, funerals, baptisms, hospital visits, teaching, and benevolence. A campus pastor can develop ministry leaders under his authority that he trains in these areas to relieve him of much of this responsibility as these are for the most part transferable. However, as pastor he still owns the responsibility of how competently they are carried out.

3.   Can he be a great clean-up pitcher?

In our paradigm, the campus pastor does not have the responsibility of preaching on a regular basis. It is however his responsibility to make a personal invitation at the end of a sermon that connects it to his local setting. We do give a campus pastor one series a year to preach. This gives him an opportunity to address a spiritual need that might only apply to his campus in a more comprehensive way. In any case, he must be able to communicate effectively in facilitating the weekend service, other important local meetings or ministries, and in any written or electronic format.

4.   Does he have the management skills to run his campus?

The campus pastor oversees the professional aspects of his and the church's ministry. He is responsible for running an effective office environment by managing the staff, the budget, and the delicate balance of time for ministry and family. He does this by establishing boundaries in time, morality, and priority for his staff. He should example this by his own life and spiritual walk. He would be encouraged to lead with his strengths and look to fill weakness gaps with new hires or volunteers.

5. Does he have the people skills to motivate his congregation?

As the recognized leader of a local congregation, the campus pastor will regularly have to manage and resolve conflict biblically and gracefully. He will be encouraging his people to step up to more critical roles of responsibility. He will use his example as a means of building respect as he leads and as he follows. He will make it a priority to effectively lead from the second chair as he submits to the authority of the senior leader and/or leadership. His voice will be the most sought after for encouragement, appreciation, and positive feedback at his campus.

Put all of these ingredients together and simmer them in the DNA of the church for a while. Take your time on this one. Even though multi-site strategy thankfully has some grace associated with it, be careful not to rely on it. In a recent conversation with Steve Gillen, Willow Creek's multi-site pastor, I heard about a proposed new multi-site launch they had been working on for some time. Just a few weeks before the launch, the leadership decided that their choice for campus pastor wasn't going to work out. Although pulling the plug on the project was disheartening, especially because of the investment of time and energy, it was better then than later. As I shared our Kirksville story with Steve, we saw a lot of commonalities. The major difference was the timing of figuring out the problem. Although the Willow Creek experience could be considered a failure, it is far easier to deal with as it comes, rather than waiting. Develop competencies that you are looking for in a campus pastor and be willing to take the time to measure a candidate against them. A new campus can take a lot in starting up and taking its first steps, but the campus pastor is the anchor point.

3rd Hurdle: Choose a Ministry Location

A ministry location can look like almost anything. Because of architectural and zoning constraints and how that affects the expansion of their parent campus, the Frederick location of Rocky Mount Christian Church is an example of a multi-million dollar solution. On the other end of the spectrum, Dave Browning of Christ the King Community Church considers it to be a campus anywhere he can get a group to form. They even have conducted GPS church. They simply put out the location of a meeting place on GPS and have people find the location themselves. It might be in any public place, moving from week to week. This has the lowest impact from a facilities point of view.

Micropolitan communities tend to have a certain niche for facilities that differ from urbanized areas in cost, availability, and visibility. Our experience is that there are options for purchasing pre-owned facilities designed for other functions that can be adapted for church use. Smaller Wal-Marts have been abandoned for super Wal-Marts. Other similar buildings have moved business in similar ways. This might apply to a grocery, home improvement, or furniture store; simple boxes with posts that can be adapted easily with great, well-lit parking lots and exposure to main roads. They are often in areas of town that city planners would like to see revitalized and often have adequate existing plumbing, electrical, and HVAC systems. Embracing an industrial look can minimize upgrade costs. One just needs to look at the community real estate with an open and creative mind.

The bigger question is deciding how big a splash you want to make and who you want to get wet. Being in a different community may mean that there is little in name recognition with the parent church, so brand exposure will have to come from different means. One strategy that creates this exposure is revitalization, potentially a big plus in a micropolitan. City fathers are always concerned about making the community better. Revitalization creates a partnership with a community, eases zoning restrictions with city planning commissions, and might even open up financial help with opportunities like enterprise zones. The only roadblock we have met in this strategy has been the loss of tax revenue to the city because of the tax-exempt status of being a church. Box stores usually occupy prime real estate on main thoroughfares that generate tax big taxes but if the city is faced with an empty building long term, it might sacrifice that revenue for the betterment of the community. While some areas are booming and real estate might have financial and zoning prohibitions, revitalization may free a church up to explore more opportunities. Using a location that needs revitalization will tighten your ministry focus as well. Locations in economically depressed areas might open up ministry doors of benevolence. Locations in ethnic areas might present cultural or bilingual opportunities. It may also close some doors. Choosing a location in an affluent part of the community might generate better giving numbers and a healthier bottom line, but might also limit opportunities in key ministry areas. These affluent areas will also come with more restrictions, greater costs, and a more difficult launch.

Here is one example of the power of this concept. The Pontiac Silverdome in Michigan recently sold. The arena holds over 80,000 seats and sits on 127 acres of land. The cost of construction was 55.7 million dollars to taxpayers 35 years ago. How much did it go for? $583,000.00! Think about how much ministry that could be done in that location and how big a splash that would make! When Lakewood Church bought the Compaq Center in Houston in 2005 for ministry, I'm sure some people considered them crazy. Now, Lakewood Church is the largest church of any kind in North America, eclipsing the next closest churches with weekend service attendance at a whopping 43,500! The second largest church is Lifechurch.tv, a multi-site pioneer that started in a former bicycle factory. With a weekend attendance in 13 locations of 26,800, Lifechurch.tv has embraced this concept. Their south Oklahoma City location is located in a former Wal-mart and was running over 2000 within 6 months. Although these examples are metropolitan, there is a lesson we can learn from them. They made a big splash that paid off. Adapting the idea in a micropolitan stands to make an even bigger one.

One great thing about micropolitans is proximity; everything is close to everything else. This includes people, ethnic groups, and economic social structures as well. This proximity makes many location issues common to metropolitan environments more or less irrelevant. Curb appeal is a lower priority, as is traffic access. Micropolitans appreciate the simplicity that reflects financial responsibility. They also appreciate the amount of investment a church is willing to make for the sake of their community. It shows a high level of seriousness and selflessness that they connect with.

If a multi-site is close enough to the parent church to connect with their reputation and branding, the name itself can make the splash. This lowers the bar on the expense or size of the facility, opening up other options to smaller venues. One might want to look at a cost to decision ratio. While it may sound great to have a church of 800 established for a facility cost of $1.5 million dollars, a church of 300 in a facility that costs $150,000.00 sounds much better with this ratio in mind. The cost to decision ration is nearly 4 times higher in the first one, $1,875.00 to $500.00! Before that sounds too good for you, realize that it is, at least at some level. In order to maintain brand, there must be a certain level of space, staff, excellence in programming, technology, and amenity. Watering the brand down too much to keep costs down will diminish impact and damage the reputation that is so valuable. This especially applies to an extension campus in the same micropolitan that can focus on a specific ministry while relying on the parent campus to be the full service location.

4th Hurdle: Figure Out a Funding Strategy

Multi-site locations are back loaded financially with high up-front costs and a space of time before receiving a return on investment. The parent church needs to be sound enough to cover the facility, improvement, and staffing costs not only up to start-up but also substantially after that. Our turn around time to a multi-site covering its own expenses is about 2 years. Discussions with other multi-site leaders confirm this to be a good rule of thumb, expecting that good cost controls are in place. Offerings when the campus starts up are usually less than half of their need. We would figure costs of construction/rehabilitation and staff costs, then add the diminishing deficit for the first two years of operation. The parent church needs to be healthy enough financially to manage this effectively.

If purchasing or raising capital debt is cost prohibitive, leasing is another option. Menlo Park Presbyterian Church in California can't afford to purchase property for its multi-sites because of the extremely high real estate costs. For them, leasing is a great option. It is a good solution to reduce capital debt to contents and build out costs. Many multi-sites locate in leased facilities like schools or community centers. While this might be cost effective, it definitely reduces the splash in a micropolitan. It seriously limits its market value to the community since it might convey that it might not be here to stay. More money would need to be spent to reverse this knee jerk attitude and prove stability. If purchasing is the best option, then securing the funds is going to be the next step. I refer you to "debt" section earlier in this book for this.

5th Hurdle: Organize the Process

Our process from conception to campus took about a year for large campuses and about 6 months for extension campuses. Developing a launch calendar with specific targets moves the process forward. Responsibilities to meet those targets need to be divided between present staff and leadership. After funding is secured, a construction manager would develop a floor plan along with leadership and present it for cost analysis. We have often done this with a volunteer that has expertise in the construction field. He would develop his own targeted calendar within the larger one, blending permitting, sub-contractor schedules, and various completion dates. Our tech team would need to examine the location and develop a technical production and I.T. plan. We would need to determine what options are available regarding bandwidth for live multi-site technology. Later on the calendar, dates would be determined for construction start to expected completion. Another team would begin the process of searching for the best staff for the new campus and when to start the hiring process. A launch date would represent the best possible time during the year with respect to the community to get maximum exposure. Leadership would be in constant review of the progress to make sure the critical targets on the calendar remained achievable or were changed early to minimize confusion. Another team would review the best approach for marketing the new location to the community.

The Crossing has taken a number of different approaches to marketing our church to its community. The best part of the approach is simply exploiting the fact that its micropolitan. A town of 20,000 people is interested in its own happenings. As soon as we took possession of the property, we had people available to lead tours, exploiting the natural curiosity of the community. During each impromptu tour, we had an opportunity to cast our vision and share our excitement for our church and the community. We held community functions like carnivals and hog roasts in our parking lot while the construction was going on, meeting new people and developing relationships. In a micropolitan, direct contact is far better than direct mail. As people came through, we gathered email information to send them updates on our progress. Using local contractors and developing relationships with them also proved invaluable as a tool of evangelism. Because of being micropolitan, the local newspapers and other media considered us legitimate news. Our projects have been on the front pages of our papers and the lead stories on the news many times. The cost of marketing is greatly reduced by these micropolitan strategies, and what planned marketing we did do was greatly enhanced by them.

6th Hurdle: Additional Staffing

Once again, I refer you to the sections earlier in this book that apply to hiring internally and externally, and in this section to the critical role of the campus pastor. Each time we start a new campus, we look to our present staff first to see if there is a passion in them to go. This is a great opportunity to fix problems or present options with present staff that may be struggling with chemistry. It may provide a chance to explore passion in a new area. Many of our staff work in a far different ministry than they were originally hired for. We just discovered their passion and made a place for them in it. We believe in exploiting that passion to its greatest extent, realizing that it is viral in nature, spreading to everyone that staff member has contact with. While such a move may create a hole in another area of ministry, I would much rather work for a new hire there and see the potential of the released passion of a present staffer in a new area. We also look to volunteers who show the kind of potential to be staff members. We poll our staff to see professionals they know who might be interested in our new location. We incorporate interns into roles under the eyes of the newly forming staff. As we move through the process of interviewing, creative thinking, and praying, God begins showing us the right direction. In the multi-site, local staff chemistry is absolutely essential to effective ministry. Chemistry is more important to us than ability. In sociology, there is a term that describes what we look for. It's called emergence. It means that a group is more than the sum of its parts. There is something that rises up out of a group in unified effort. You can see it at a ball game, a worship service, a mission trip, or in a great staff. A multi-site staff is like a family, dependent on one another for success, encouragement, and support. When the chemistry is right, the organization gets more than just the sum of their work.

The order of hiring is important as it helps establish chemistry and loyalty. We always seek to hire the campus pastor first, involving him in the initial steps of the new launch. He is involved in each additional hire, the second being the worship pastor. While the campus pastor is the most critical link, because of the nature of the multi-site and a single preacher, the worship pastor is the face that the congregation sees the most. Since each location conducts its own worship, his style of worship will shape much of the local DNA. This makes him the second most critical hire. We also hire a children's pastor first and launch student ministry a few months after the initial launch. Our style of worship connects with students so youth groups can follow initial start-up, however, children from 0 through 12 are very high priorities at launch. If possible, we stretch volunteers from existing campuses to work in the new campus until new volunteers can be established. We do this for two reasons:

1. We have a certain importable way of doing ministry in these areas that our present volunteers are familiar with.

2. We want the young church to develop as a family in worship together for the first few months together.

Our 4th hire is the one that holds everything together. It is a full-time administrative assistant. We who call ourselves pastors would simply be lost without them. Finally, we hire someone in the area of technology to be responsible to run those aspects of services and help with I.T.

7th Hurdle: Launch

Launch is the culmination of the calendar: the last of the targets. As the formal introduction of the church to the community, it is the most critical first impression, so it has to be our best effort. We always encourage a large group from existing campuses to attend the new campus for the first few weeks to instill the DNA into the new congregation. Since the micropolitan paradigm is a completely new and unfamiliar approach to doing church in the community, the members of the existing locations teach the new group the parent church's approach by showing them how to sing, celebrate, worship, and respond. Newly attracted people need permission to express themselves, as they are unfamiliar with church boundaries. The launch gets them familiar with their surroundings too. Checking in their children to others gives them their first experience into the various facets of this new ministry. The whole experience of walking in, meeting and mingling with new people, finding familiar faces, and experiencing worship is completely fresh. The environment brings down defenses as attenders find something they didn't expect.

The launch is the first impression and as such is absolutely crucial to establishing hundreds of first-time relationships. It gives the church the opportunity to expand its data base for follow up through children's sign-ups, filling out an information flap in the service, or signing up for more information. Compiling and managing that data over the first few weeks gives the staff an opportunity to see what the shape of the new congregation is so as to make any adjustments necessary. There are going to be plenty of questions and feedback requiring a response as a church establishes itself and its brand. It needs to be a time of clarity instead of confusion in the area of DNA. There will be plenty of other things that don't work exactly as they are supposed to, requiring troubleshooters from other campuses to be on sight to handle whatever comes up so that local staff can concentrate on relationship development. We have had everything from computer check-in glitches to toilets backing up. The last thing a campus pastor needs to worry about at this time is these kinds of problems.

If like us, your multi-site uses the preaching of a single pastor and location, the sermon series selected will also be an important component to launch. When we launched Macomb, we began a new series called "Dashboard Jesus". It centered on moving our faith from a plastic, iconic religious duty to a full time, meaningful relationship. It was really a multi-week examination of our vision to help people find an intimate personal relationship with Jesus Christ. The bumper music was John Bon Jovi's *Lost Highway*. The praise music came out hard hitting with a guitar solo and was unapologetically loud with video, lights, and haze. The experience defined the new location and staff as micropolitan, a complete change from church as usual, focusing primarily outward and downward. That first church service will repel some people, but they will be predominately churchgoers already, and not the primary target. Those attracted will be that target and will want to share their new discovery with everyone they know. The launch is not a time to be afraid of mistakes, as the new church really has nothing to compare it to that even comes close.

8th *Hurdle: Metrics*

In a multi-site strategy, metrics are required to measure the individual components of programming and the new micropolitan as a whole. The choices of specific programming will need to fit the local setting. Multi-sites have both a local and regional personality so some aspects of measurement will already be established and others will need to be developed locally. *Our first multi-site campus pastor mentioned recently that the most important metric they had for the first two years was simply to survive.* As a new church paradigm, the multi-site strategy is really very young and comprehensive information about failures are mostly anecdotal but they remind us that the risks are high. Lifechurch.tv builds a multi-site model that needs to run 2000 to be sustainable. Our micropolitan model for stand-alone campuses in a community is about 700-800 in weekly attendance. Below that, the local body will still be on some measure of life support. Viability models out there run the table with regard to size of congregation expected, amount of paid staff, technological sophistication, and square footage necessary. Since we want to give the feel of a megachurch, there are certain minimums in these areas that we feel need to be present and these numbers achieve it.

There are four key metrics we use to measure viability:

1. Attendance

Since we export people from other campuses during start-up, being able to track attendance starts out a bit sketchy with early attendance numbers somewhat inflated. Before long, that inflated number will level out to provide a clearer picture of what the new campus actually looks like. Having 700 to 800 people creates enough opportunity for multiple services, an adequate volunteer ministry pool, an adequate number of locally musically talented people, and a spiritual energy level to fuel continued attraction. Because attendance is the primary generator and first measurable number for the rest of the metrics, we put an early focus on it.

Attendance speaks volumes about quality in areas like attraction, invitation, and barriers that need to be addressed. Any growing church will face lids to growth. They are most often seen as a leveling out of attendance. Lids may be encountered because the organization is maxed out or a ministry leader has reached his "peter principle", reaching a level of incompetence. They may be encountered because the church is just taking a breath, getting used to itself. They also may occur when there is sin in the church, particularly in the leadership.

Some of most obvious attendance lids we have encountered have turned out to be because of sin. Make no mistake, launching a church and the associated high expectations is a high stress experience and staffers burn the candle at both ends. The spiritual weakness that comes from these high levels can be very dangerous, so high levels of accountability are critical in these stressful times. In every launch, there are going to be failures. It would be naive to think that we could avoid them all. It's what we do after those failures that will determine what we will be. Some of these failures just need counseling. Others are too damaging for just that and require termination. Any time of these major failures present themselves, Satan takes a calculated risk. He expects that the church will try to minimize damage by covering it up, letting it go away quietly. Proverbs 14:12 says, "There is a way that seems right to man, but the end thereof is the way of death." Nowhere is that more true than in the church. When sin is exposed to the light, Satan has gotten all he is going to get. If the church takes the way of truth and handles it with grace, God will lift the lid and the church will continue to move forward.

Jerry Harris

2. Finances

There is a synergy between attendance and giving when a measure of time is added to it. Our break-even numbers are usually found in $10-15 per capita giving at our multi-sites. We gauge ourselves to reasonable expectations that may seem low, but it needs to be understood that being so intentional about reaching outside of the churched world and having a concentration on an economically challenged part of the community will mean a lower number. It has usually taken between 18 months and 2 years for giving to catch general fund giving up with attendance. Generating between $8,000.00 and $9,000.00 per week supports a $1.5 million debt retirement, 4 to 5 full time staff, and usual ministry expenses.

Our experience in giving at multi-sites have started out somewhere between 40%-50% of need. As the congregation begins to take ownership of the location and invests their time and talent in ministry, giving starts to rise. The parent church needs to realize that there will be a period of time that the location will be in deficit spending as it finds its footing and budgets its funds accordingly. Like attendance, if lids are encountered in giving, the reasons are likely similar. Giving is a spiritual discipline and as such, will not be one of the first things a new believer learns. An outward focus will slow this process at first, but later it will catch up as long as expectations remain realistic. Reaching the giving metric and establishing the leadership metric at the same time, around the 2-year mark, has worked best for us. Once a congregation is giving over its need, it wants to have a voice in how and on who that money is spent.

3. Ministries

A stand-alone campus is defined here as one that is not intended to continually require support as a mission or be specifically targeted like an extension campus. It is a primary church location for a micropolitan, looking not only to meet it's own needs, but to partner with other viable campuses to continue the movement to new micropolitans. Because it stands alone in the community, it is required to have all necessary ministries represented and running well. This applies to all age related ministries from early childhood through senior high, an aggressive discipleship program of small groups, and volunteer ministry teams for services.

The Crossing runs on its ministry volunteers. They make up virtually all the necessary teams that meet a church's responsibility, a family's needs, and a newcomer's first impression. The staff would be totally ineffective without them. The multi-site metric is measured as volunteers from other campuses are peeled off and replaced with local volunteers. When there is a healthy rotation to prevent ministry burnout comprised of only local volunteers, the multi-site has met its viability metric.

4. Leadership

Unlike many multi-site models that are exclusively staff led, the Crossing believes in a partnership of leadership between paid staff and local lay leaders. Paul instructed Timothy to appoint elders in every church, giving him guidelines in their choosing. Each multi-site campus pastor begins targeting potential leaders from that first weekend, looking like Timothy for those who will carry the wonderful burden along with him. This process of finding local leaders takes longer than the rest of the metrics because it takes time to get a sense of confidence in whether potential leaders meet biblical criteria and also have the chemistry needed for unity. Your leadership structure may be different, but regardless a metric of leadership remains necessary.

Once two leaders are considered fit for leadership, the campus pastor will make recommendation to the existing

Jerry Harris

eldership. They are presented to the congregation for any spiritual objection. Without objection, they are voted on and installed as part of the eldership. We have a single eldership that represents all of our stand- alone campuses. Once these elders are installed at the local campus, the metric has been met. The Crossing organizational structure is represented in two intersecting circles. One circle is made up of senior staff and the other are the elders of the church. The senior pastor is the link between the eldership and the staff. One of his primary responsibilities is to maintain the confidence of each group in the other. Campus pastors are on the senior staff and are invited to meetings of the eldership. This structure has served us well as we have moved forward with multi-site. People have a sense of representation and communication. We feel that this model is critical for being one church in multiple locations. It also avoids a feel of mini-denominationalism that can be inherent with the multi-site model.

Parody

While parody is not a metric that we look at for viability, it is nonetheless considered and addressed. It wasn't very long after establishing our first multi-site campus that staff members at the new site began to complain about not having the same bells and whistles as the parent campus. This problem was compounded when starting up additional campuses. Staffers and volunteers would see something in a ministry area that they didn't have and question the fairness of it. We quickly needed to define that all multi-sites don't have to be exactly the same. Some communities lend themselves to be more invested in a particular ministry than others. Sometimes, the facility itself dictates a difference in resources than the others. Sometimes it's the success of a program that requires more resources. It's easy to see why there might be some hard feelings produced. We constantly face issues in budgeting that force us to prioritize the many good ideas, programs, and capital improvement. Much of our branding or DNA has a certain look and package of ministries associated with it, so a certain amount of parody is something we seek after. There just needs to be clear communication of why one location might receive something that another doesn't have. Campuses can be like children, each calling the other 'the favorite child' depending on the circumstance. Getting the senior staff and elders on the same page with regard to prioritization is vitally important for the senior pastor of a multi-site church to consider.

Multi-site Benefits

Multi-site Turbo Charges Growth

Micropolitan communities with generally stagnant population statistics are hardly a place to expect exponential growth, but when a ministry approach connects with its people, the unexpected will happen. Multi-site strategy increases that growth potential by amount of campuses and experiences. The church has known for a long time that adding multiple services in one location increases attendance dramatically. Now imagine adding a multiplier of 2, 3, 4, or 5 to that potential. Each campus launched and each new experience offered has kept us growing constantly. Complete strangers regularly remind me when I attend our multi-sites how powerfully God is working through them. While risks are high and challenges are plentiful every time we reach out to a new venue, the victories serve to remind us just how worth it it is. In 2009, the Crossing was the fastest growing church of all Independent Christian Churches and was Outreach Magazine's 27th fastest growing church of any kind in America. Those accomplishments are a reflection of the way the multi-site strategy turbo charges growth and impact. Remember, all of this has happened in predominantly stagnant communities as it applies to population growth. Just imagine what might happen in the communities around your church as a vibrant micropolitan.

Multi-site Makes a Regional Impact

As you explore different means and methods in the pursuit of a vision, and those ideas become realities, new opportunities form out of them that would have never been seen otherwise. When we chose to become a multi-site church, it never occurred to us that we would become a regional one. A micropolitan multi-site church has learned to think beyond the influence of one community to more than a few. As sites are added and church growth multiplies, a relationship forms around the spheres of influence of each site as they intersect one another. It becomes exciting to think about how strategically placing campuses regionally in order to blanket the entire area with an easy driving distance to a location and the establishing local small groups can increase the influence of a church.

Although we didn't envision the church regionally, once we saw it, we got excited about it. Creating a map that shows population concentration and how that relates to present multi-site locations can go a long way to pinpoint future locations or extensions.

Multi-site Opens Up Partnering Opportunities

The multi-site model forces multi-dimensional, non-linear thinking. Recently, we had twenty-three Southern Baptist pastors from the state association come to visit us and glean any ideas that appealed to them. One of the pastors took me aside and asked, "Why would you even want to do this in the first place?" It seemed more like a headache to him than anything else. As I explained my passion to reach beyond the limits of one community, he was at a loss. I don't blame him. It is just an example of two dimensional, linear thinking. Multi-site is exponential thinking, not being limited to addition and subtraction, but expanding to multiplication and division.

There are a number of ways that multi-dimensional thinking interfaces with a multi-site church beyond the establishment of new sites. Multi-site churches attract the attention of churches at all stages of development. They may be trying to get a good start, struggling to grow, concentrating on self-preservation, or dead in the water. When they hear about the rapid growth, the spiritual health, the advanced technology, and the willingness a multi-site church has to reach out to help other church bodies with their needs, they might be open to some sort of defined partnership. This is a great opportunity for a Kingdom-minded multi-site church to impact needy churches for the greater good and an awesome opportunity for any church willing to learn.

The Crossing approaches these partnering opportunities five different ways:

Resourcing

We believe that whatever we have developed belongs to the whole Kingdom so we are happy to share free access to all of our materials from sermon series, small group material, youth ministry material and ideas, structural concepts, and training means or methods.

Consulting

We are happy to speak to and encourage discussions with all of our departments via phone, ichat, email, or a scheduled face-to-face visit as it fits into various schedules.

Coaching

Coaching is for those who simply want a second opinion or an outside set of eyes to evaluate your church and give some ideas for changes you may want to make. Although we have a "Crossing" way, coaching is not designed to make you one of us. It helps you evaluate programming, staff, leadership, facility, culture, services, mission, vision, core values, volunteer base, evangelism, discipleship, retention, technology, and giving.

Partnering

Some may want their campus to look and feel like the Crossing but still retain their name and leadership. We would conduct comprehensive evaluation and analysis of the above church components and help you formulate an action plan to manage the changes.

Merging

This is for those churches who would want to become a Crossing campus. This would require a release of control of all aspects of the campus as we work together to create a positive transition.

These are just short definitions of different forms of partnership we are exploring and the particulars are much more in depth than related here. However, you can see that there are all sorts of possibilities when we don't limit ourselves to linear thinking.

Different forms of partnering open up all sorts of potential opportunities for a multi-site micropolitan church. There are people managing all sorts of unused resources like buildings, land, or people in the Kingdom just looking for a way to bring new life into their community or church. Just think of all the underutilized resources in the Kingdom of God that could be coached, consulted, redirected, or acquired to make a difference once again in a fresh, new way! Multi-dimensional thinking lifts lids of limitation to any church not only willing to think outside the box, but envision themselves in all sorts of new boxes.

Multi-site Can Go International

I've never worked with a church that didn't have a foreign mission budget. In the past, my personal experience with mission budgets has been line after line of token support to mission works all over the world. I think most churches like the idea of having some measure of impact in as many places as possible. This takes the pressure off the local church since a mission point can lose their support without much financial impact, but it puts more pressure on the missionary to maintain contact and visit a lot more churches when stateside. In the last few decades, some churches have moved to more substantial support to fewer missions, even considering going "living link" as the primary supporter of the missionary or a particular aspect of the mission.

The multi-site approach can take the mission emphasis of a church to a completely new place of ownership and involvement. If the church has already determined to be a primary supporter of a mission, it isn't that big a leap financially to consider a higher level of ownership of that mission. Just putting the name of the supporting church on the mission creates ties to the congregation. It builds in a desire to see the mission prosper and receive whatever needs it has for greater effectiveness. It also develops a higher sense of accountability for the mission. As discussed in the following chapter, for many foreign missions, out of sight is out of mind. A stronger connection using multi-site tools aids a mission in staying on task.

The Crossing developed its international emphasis through a hire for the Quincy campus. Through a third party connection of one of our staff members, we became aware of a South African family that was interested in coming to the states to do ministry. Barry and Ine' Stander sold nearly all their earthy possessions to come to America. They were an incredible team for children's ministry with off the chart creativity. They did incredible ministry for three years, but when the time was winding down on their visas, they had to decide whether to pursue naturalization or return to their country. Barry approached me with an idea to start a Crossing campus in Mosselbay, South Africa. It was a city roughly the same size as ours on the coast between Port Elizabeth and Cape Town. Our goal was to become the only fully integrated church in the city, utilizing the benefits of multi-site and a shared vision.

Within a year, the Crossing Mosselbay was running between 100 and 200 in attendance. They utilize our sermons downloaded from iTunes weekly. We have sent one of our staff to be their full-time youth minister from the Quincy campus. They are the only fully integrated church in the area and have an aggressive ministry to the surrounding townships.

While language and culture would undoubtedly be barriers in many ministry areas, the resourcing, ownership, and accountability takes on new meaning if they are perceived as a mission campus. While there are obstacles that really don't work internationally, for example finances, other advantages available through technology are transferable and translatable. We are presently purchasing property in Chennai, India and partnering with an already established body of believers for a new campus there.

Think about the mission points that your church supports and the amount of impact that is untapped because of the distance. One of the greatest assets of today's technology is how it makes time and distance less relevant. It's an awesome thought to harness it for the Kingdom of God.

Part 6: Micromissional Vision

Living the Beatitudes

Nathan Rector, the Crossing's previous pastor of Discipleship was sharing an approach to a new sermon series called "Living Black and White in a Gray World" based on the Sermon on the Mount. As he studied the text, something never seen before began to emerge. *In the first four beatitudes, Jesus emphasizes actions that promote emptiness.* Being poor in spirit comes from an understanding of our need for His Spirit and the long ago death of our own. Mourning is the result of recognition and repentance of sin. Meekness is attained as we eliminate pride and arrogance. Hungering and thirsting for righteousness is the inevitable result, a picture of an empty heart longing to be filled.

The next three beatitudes reveal how God would have us fill that emptiness. Showing mercy is the first component that God would see our hearts filled with. It is to be followed by a pure heart, possessed with motives exclusively for the honor of God. Finally, making peace finishes the filling. The result of a heart filled this way is shown as full of righteousness that can withstand the persecution that comes from it.

Our world is not an empty place. Like our hearts, it is filled with all sorts of things that distract us, pollute our souls, and leave our lives complicated, confused, and defeated. When we allow the Holy Spirit to convict us, an emptying process begins. It produces a hunger for filling, but with something good and right. When we live missionally, their emptying is our filling. The Holy Spirit works through us both for sowing and reaping. Receiving mercy requires humility, admitting to the state of our lives produces mourning, demolishing the strongholds and defense mechanisms of people in pain produces meekness. As we reach out to minister in these ways to hurting people and their hearts begin to pour out the unnecessary, we have the opportunity to show mercy, evaluate the purity of our motives, and make peace in a troubled heart.

With these concepts in mind, the idea of how to accomplish the "mission" might begin to come into focus, but there are plenty of ideas that may already be rattling around in our heads. These perceptions and the programs that flow from them could probably use a fresh look as we seek to give Jesus to the world.

The Mission is More Than "Foreign"

Growing up in the church, the word "mission" conjured up pictures of jungles and natives, people in desperation needing the western touch. Missionaries would be armed with slide projectors, tables of trinkets, and a powerful motive appeal fueled by mostly pity. I went to a mission centered Bible college in preparation for the ministry. The approach was pretty much the same. The term "mission" was almost exclusively a foreign field idea with only a few domestic exceptions. As I began to form my worldview, I challenged the term "missions" with the professor over the department. I explained that the word "mission" should always be singular because the church has only one mission, whether it happens across the world or across the fence.

Even though he considered my viewpoint anti-mission, nothing could be further from the truth for me. God's financial blessings to America demand a response from the church to the developing world. I have participated in some incredible works on the foreign field, but more than a quarter century in local ministry has been a long lesson in a battle against cynicism. My affiliation has been with a primarily independent, non-denominational church without much in the way of oversight, probably reacting to the potential for corruption with too much power. Nowhere is the weakness inherent with independence and absence of oversight seen more than in foreign mission works. Out of sight is out of mind in many overseas works. With no one to set the bar, difficulties inherent with these fields become excuses for a lowering of the bar. Without a more direct oversight than a board on the other side of the world can give, it becomes easy to just maintain. Once again, cynically, I have noticed that the mission field has become a potential catch all for people who want to be in ministry but lack the skills to accomplish a return on investment. Sending then serves two pragmatic purposes in the church: 1) It provides an outlet for under talented people to call themselves professionals in the Kingdom of God, and 2) It eases the church's sense of responsibility for the lost world without becoming any more directly involved than writing a check and providing a job.

My battle with cynicism hasn't been made any easier with some of the scandals connected to the foreign mission field I have seen. Misappropriation of funds, sexual misconduct, false reporting, and politics have been every bit as prevalent on the mission field as it is at home. The same weaknesses that promote exploitation domestically are there on the mission field, but without regular visual and financial accountability, the dangers are very real. My worship pastor just returned from the border of Uganda and Sudan. He has a passion for encouraging indigenous missionaries in the most persecuted areas of the world. They told him that American money had done more to harm the cause of Christ than to help it. It had been intercepted, misappropriated, and used to promise hope only to dash it shortly after, doing more to incite violence than to bring people to Jesus. Our good intentions are not an adequate defense when so much is at stake.

Now don't get me wrong! I'm not saying that we should stay away from the foreign mission field, however, I am saying that the same level of accountability that we apply domestically is absolutely critical to bring honor and glory to the name of Jesus. We must be diligent to tear down the excuses that we use to give us license to do sub-standard work. Even then, we can't step away from our own responsibility to carry out the mission of the church by simply sending others to do it, accountable or not. The commission of the mission is universal. So where do I go? How do I make disciples? Who do I baptize? What do I teach? The micropolitan community shows us a mission field everyday, but do we see it?

The Mission is All Around Us

The mission is all around us, in every moment, every experience, every idle word, every mundane task! The reason that mission has to be redefined in the singular is that we cannot let go of our personal responsibility to make a difference in another life. I know churches that have great mission programs to places all over the world but very little or nothing to reach out to the people right around them. *I wonder if we just like to keep our hands clean by writing a check rather than extending one to lift someone up.* It is so much easier to do that or take the short-term mission trip that you get to come home from, thankful for the distance, than to be up close and personal with a hurting person on a more daily basis. It should give us pause. A commitment too close to just walk away from is much more intimidating and has a lot more potential to mess

175

up what might seem to be a well-ordered life. I can certainly see why many have seen the church as somewhat irrelevant in this area. Many churches today have grown cynical about the hurt around them. As I mentioned before, a Christian radio station in Quincy was advertising a local church in our area. The ad encouraged people to try out their church if they would like to join with other "stable families". I remember feeling so much anger the first time I heard that ad. This many years in ministry has taught me that there is really no such thing as a "stable family", just people who hide their particular pain better than others. Churches turn away from this pain jaded by those who play the system.

Recently, one such person took advantage of a number of the elderly in our church. She had a propensity for writing bad checks. She came to church as she was tied up with her charges in the courts. Two particular couples stayed with her through her sentencing, prison time, and were waiting for her when her time was done. They helped to set her up in her own house, found her multiple jobs, and worked to put her life back together. After so much help, she extorted more than $13,000.00 from her new job and went back to prison, probably for the rest of her life. It wasn't hard to grow cynical about reaching out after her negative influence.

But we cannot turn away just because of the certainty of being taken advantage of. Jesus taught us that our "hands on" compassion is what God will use to judge us. His words in Luke 6:37-38 make it clear that God will use **our** standard of measurement. In verse 38, Jesus says, "For with the measure you use, it will be measured to you." If we are cynical to the hurt around us, God will use our standard of cynicism to judge us. Matthew 25:31-46 teaches us that ministering to the people hurting around us is no different than ministering to Jesus Himself. Jesus uses words to paint a collage of tragedy defined by the hungry and thirsty, strangers and the ragged, the sick and incarcerated. We know that many broken people in micropolitan communities have figured out how to make the circuit, playing on the tender hearts of the church, on the con for the next meal or drink, just trying to survive.

Crossing the Bridge of Pain

Pain is a powerful teacher, albeit a difficult one. The idea of "mission" is in many ways born out of pain and the needs it produces. Those of us experiencing the fullness of life in Christ presuppose a spiritual pain that comes from an empty place within, only satisfied by being filled with Him. We also see ministry to physical, mental, or emotional pain as a bridge to be crossed in order to minister to the deeper spiritual pain. We are all aware of the pictures of poverty, disease, and ignorance that fuel our desire to reach out and embrace "mission". But pain is not limited to the starving that require the $20 monthly sponsorship. It takes many forms and produces opportunities close to home as well as overseas.

The way we reach out to hurting people is an incredible opportunity for the micropolitan church to set itself apart from the rank and file. Ministering to people, especially those outside the church, in the midst of their difficulties with our own hands connects us to how Jesus did it Himself. He certainly didn't need to make mud from spitting in the dust to rub on a man's eyes. He could have healed a leper from a safe distance. He could have spoken to a tax collector in the street rather than to invite himself over for lunch. The depth of His compassion was experienced in the up-close interaction. While it is obviously a good thing to support missions on a foreign field, I think it should mirror the mission we are accomplishing in our own back yards. I John 4:20 tells us, "If anyone says "I love God" yet hates his brother, he is a liar. For anyone who does not love his brother, whom he has seen, cannot love God, whom he has not seen." These aren't only people on the other side of the world, they are also the ones we either see or avoid everyday.

The pain that people are experiencing all around us gives us an opportunity to share with them in meaningful, tangible ways that help them to see the relevance of a relationship with Jesus Christ. The benefit of a micropolitan is once again in its proximity. Because the community is smaller geographically, the mission is right in front of us or just down the street. When we get close to this kind of pain, it will evoke a response that either moves our hearts to minister, or repels us from ministering. The attitude we exhibit reflects what might be going on in our hearts.

I remember Susan's story, a woman who had been raped and abused most of her life. The first time I met her in the church lobby, she did her best to avoid me, and for that matter everyone else. When I crossed the distance to talk to her, she kept her head down and mumbled the few words she spoke in response. I found out later that she was ashamed to speak because her teeth were gone. As her story unfolded in Celebrate Recovery, I found out that her teeth were not just gone, they had been knocked out by her ex-husband, just the latest in a seemingly endless string of abuse. Our men's ministry heard the story and because men had been responsible for most of the tragedy of her life, they decided to take responsibility and pay for her to have new dental implants. I will never forget the day she came up to me after the procedure. Her smile lit up the lobby! She later told me that when the oral surgeon handed her the mirror to see her new smile, she felt God take the pain of all that abuse out of her heart. Stories like Susan's are certainly inspiring but it takes more than inspiration to make "missional" the norm for a church.

Pain Moves Us All

What does the micromissional field look like? In a church that targets a younger crowd, personal pain might center on addiction, single parenting, or divorce. In an older target, it might involve ministries surrounding issues like illness, loneliness, and death of a loved one. Just lift up your eyes…

> *"Do you not say, "Four months more and then the harvest? I tell you, open your eyes and look at the fields! They are ripe for harvest. Even now the reaper draws his wages, even now he harvests the crop for eternal life, so that the sower and the reaper may be glad together." John 4:35-36*

There are so many stories that flood my mind as I think how God has used pain to open a heart to a relationship with God. This is just one of them.

Angel and Ryan sat on the front row when they started attending the Crossing. Ryan worked for Jeff who owned a car business and had come to the Crossing some years ago, looking for relief from the pain of his addictions, trying to reattach to the faith he had felt earlier in his life. These two he had invited were a great looking young couple, smiling and outwardly very well presented. Most of us are very good at this discipline of public hypocrisy. Angel and Ryan were experts at it! It wasn't long however, that the constant encouragement people get around here for transparency got through to them and they started trusting people with their personal stories. They were living together but unmarried, both recovering from previous failures induced by various addictions leaving a trail of hurt people in the wake of their individual lives. Their life situation was made more difficult by their lack of finances. It wasn't that they didn't make any money; they just had to spend it on all the results of past poor choices.

Jerry Harris

Two years before meeting Angel and Ryan, our custodian brought me a box that had been left in our women's bathroom. Upon opening it, I found a carefully written note and a beautiful women's engagement and wedding ring. The anonymous note told of the pain of a failed marriage and related the hope of someone else using these rings for God's glory. I remember the pain attached to that note as I placed the little box in my desk drawer. Angel scheduled an appointment with me to discuss her life's difficulties. The conversation shifted to their finances and the fact that she and Ryan were convicted that they should be married but he was unwilling to ask her since he couldn't afford a proper ring. I started smiling uncontrollably, realizing that God was answering a silent prayer from two years before in the women's bathroom. I told Angel that God had provided her ring, that it was in my desk, and that Ryan should come in and get it. She began to cry. A week later, Ryan came in to get it. A couple of weeks after that, Angel and Ryan decided to give their lives to Christ and be baptized. While waiting to go into the water together, Ryan got down on his knees back stage and proposed to Angel. It was an engaged couple that was baptized that day.

That's not the end of the story. Ryan came up to me some time later and handed me a box. I opened it and saw the two rings I had given them. I found out that they weren't the same rings, just ones as close to the original ones they could find. Ryan said that the ones Angel was wearing they considered a gift from God but they wanted to pay it forward as God had turned their lives around in such a powerful way. Pain gives us an opportunity to reach people otherwise unreachable to share the love and healing of Jesus.

Pain also changes us. It forces us to take a fresh look at all the "settled" things in our lives and brings priorities into focus that may have been comfortably marginalized. Pain not only draws hurting people to a sensitive church, pain we experience opens us up to invest in ministries previously neglected. It was the pain of personal tragedy that moved Bob Buford. He was a highly successful media mogul, but the death of his son and only child was the turning point that God allowed in his life to move him from success to significance. Bob founded the Buford foundation and Leadership Network, an organization that seeks to accelerate the emergence of effective churches. He also wrote *Halftime*, a book that helps those moving through exhilarating and potentially dangerous shoals of midlife by focusing on significance instead of success. At the graveside, he said these words,

> *"God," I began, "you have given my life into my hands, I give it back to you. My time, my property, my life itself...knowing it is only an instant compared to my life with you (and with Ross) in eternity." With palms down, I concluded, "Father, to you I release the cares and concerns of this world, knowing you loved me enough to give your only Son on my behalf. I'm a sinner in need of a Savior and, once again, I accept what you have done for me as sufficient. In Jesus' name. Amen."* **14**

Bob's personal pain moved him to impact thousands of lives for Jesus. Similar situations may open our hearts to ministries never before considered as God uses the tragedies that a fallen world hands us to turn others and us toward Him.

Micropolitan + Missional = Micromissional

As mentioned before, one of great positives of being in a micropolitan community is the proximity that people have to one another. Another positive is that an aggressive approach to ministry has a much bigger impact in a smaller community. Nowhere have we experienced more profoundly the power of these two assets than by connecting micropolitan culture to the concept of "missional".

While I'm beginning to understand the concept of "missional" in a micropolitan context, I don't know if I really understand or agree with how some define it. Part of my confusion comes from its use as a buzzword born out some more recent philosophical conversations and the words and definitions that come from them. One of the most confusing, "emergent", led some great thinkers into conversations that fell away from sound teaching. Their thinking moved to redefine the church as irrelevant, truth as relative, and the Bible are errant. Rob Bell's reference to and redefinition of truth as springs on a trampoline as opposed to bricks in a wall in *Velvet Elvis* was alarming as his postmodern teaching and resources were widely accepted. Others like Brian McLaren and Tony Jones gave up on the last hope of the world: the church, along with truth in their conversation.

When those who brought the word "missional" forward, it seemed that they were making a response to the emergent movement to bring things back to truth. Still reacting to the consumerist nature of the church growth movement and the megachurch, the missional movement directed us to "be the church" instead of "going to church". The desire was to take the idea of ministry and make it real and personal by getting outside the walls of the church and just doing it. That sounded really great, but not in the absence of God's great immortal invention, the church. Some proponents of the "missional " church began to gravitate more toward social justice, losing sight of the reason behind it. Some missional advocates reduced "the mission" to just sitting down and starting up a conversation with someone at the local Starbucks or taking a more active role in reaching out one on one. While the idea of reaching out personally is crucial to the lifestyle of a self-proclaimed Christian and consistent with a Christian world view, its practice excluded from the local church almost sounds more like a capitulation to the Scriptural mandate, thinking that the church no longer knows or understands how to empower and mobilize its people to engage their culture. Seeking a new purity by "boiling down" the church into autonomous small groups that meet in houses or just living an individual Christian life is, in my opinion, an attempt to replace the New Testament model of body life and authority out of frustration. Some might argue that house churches are indeed biblical and they would be right, but not in the absence of a structure of church authority.

The letter of III John gives some specific insight into one such church. Diotrephes "who wants to be first" is working outside of the larger structure of the church. He is not in agreement with the larger church's desire to send out missionaries, not only refusing to house them, but also putting people out of the church who do so. John takes authority by speaking to Gaius, a church supporter, and brings forward Demetrius to replace Diotrephes. There is clearly a measure of structure as seen in the cooperative effort of the church to send out missionaries and a measure of authority that John is using to redirect the renegade group.

Even though "missional" might be a word that fringe groups have attempted to highjack, I think it a great word to connect to micropolitan. We are indeed called to be the church, not just go to it. The mission is not just on the other side of the world, it is no further away than our next conversation. Mobilizing the micropolitan church and its resources in an environment where there is a real potential for lasting change is more than significant. Being micromissional can help the micropolitan church make huge strides in knowing and doing the will of God intimately and personally.

The Crossing's Micomissional Story

The Crossing's micromissional emphasis was another ministry approach that we backed into more than intentionally sought out. Like most churches, we have always had a line item in our annual budget for local needs. If someone lost his or her home, we would step up with help. The occasional transient would come looking for bus fare or gas money. The occasional need for shelter would be covered or a gift card for the local Aldi store for groceries. We would be taken advantage of as often as not, so our cynicism limited our line item to $18,000.00 annually. We had a ministry team in charge of the disbursement. Even at this meager amount, we were one of the largest providers in Quincy for local benevolence.

The first place where God took us to soften our hard heart was Celebrate Recovery. Our Celebrate Recovery program got us closer to the very real pain that all sorts of people were feeling in our own community. When we started investing in the people such a program attracts, the stories connected with addictive and personally destructive behavior began to surface quickly. I need to back up a moment and tell you about hiring Jim Dennis. This hire raised the eyebrows of several people at our church. He definitely had two sides to his resume'. On the positive side, Jim was a 52-year-old former executive who was brought up in Quincy. He had been a basketball player on the high school's championship team. His family owned a lucrative business that set them up in the country club scene. He was a graduate of SMU and had a lot of experience in the business world. On the negative side, for most of his adult life, he was a highly functioning alcoholic; he had blown through 4 marriages, and never stayed with anything very long. However, even with the failures of his past, God had His hand on him for greater things. God had literally taken most everything away from him, putting in a humble state, all the while shaping him for what was to come.

I have already shared that we hire people, not positions. We do this based on concepts in Jim Collins' book *Good to Great*. We are far more concerned about getting the right people on the bus and then figure out which seat they will be the most effective in. Jim Dennis was definitely one of those hires. Jim had accepted Christ at the Crossing in the midst of the breakup of his 4th marriage. He had already gotten a handle on his alcoholism when I met him. Being a part of a more privileged crowd growing up and his connection with sports got him across many racial and economic lines. Those bridges would prove to be key with regards to God's plan for him.

Even though Jim moved out of the area, we kept in touch. He often shared his desire to serve in full-time ministry. When an option in connection with small groups opened up, we began to talk. He came to the Crossing with a heart full of passion for hurting people. It wasn't long before he approached me about Celebrate Recovery. Soon, Celebrate Recovery was his ministry focus. I could see that he was in the right place and worked hard to let him get in that right seat on the bus. God does awesome things in people's lives around here, but you would be hard pressed to see it any more vividly than in Celebrate Recovery. The contrast of the ugliness of addiction and its effect on individuals and families to the incredible look of change and redemption is breathtaking. It is a ministry where the work of the Holy Spirit and the daily battle with principalities and powers is in sharp focus. In my mind, micromissional really started here.

The real game changer didn't happen until we took that trip to Post Falls, Idaho and Real Life Ministries. Jim was one of the four of us that went. He told me later that he really felt like a fish out of water with us. We were getting coaching from Jim Putman on discipleship and how to reconstruct our ministry around it. Jim was mostly quiet, not usual for his quick wit and colorful metaphors. We heard about Real Life's benevolence outreach and how they used a thrift store to fund it. That was not why we were there or at least we thought, but Jim said he wanted to go see what they were doing while the other three of us stayed on task. He went to the thrift store, spoke with the staff, connected with their Celebrate Recovery pastor, and learned about how they meted out benevolence. With a full heart, he started to share with the rest of us.

Micropolitan communities are not usually thought of as a context for the poor and broken. Society defines poverty more in the urban context. But the truth is that the poor are in micropolitans and they are neglected even more because of the lack of local funding from either government or private sources. Like everything else, micropolitans don't have as many options. This lack of options goes well beyond choices of movies at the local cinema or different kinds of restaurants. The poor, the homeless, and the broken go as unnoticed as possible. As Jim shared what he had seen and learned, a new idea began forming to introduce a new group of people into an intimate personal relationship with Christ. We had available space in our Macomb location for a thrift store. How much would it take to open one up? How would we keep it stocked? Who would run it? Where would we find workers to operate it? How much revenue would it produce? What would we do with it? Real Life gave us a great template for a solid start as we dreamed about how many relationship opportunities God would bring through it.

What we had seen in Post Falls was not the easiest vision to cast. Even staff members were skeptical, seeing it as more of a distraction than a proper focus. One elder/staffer took it to heart. Bruce Freeman had been an elder for years but only recently had come on staff part-time for pastoral care and benevolence. It was his responsibility to investigate needs and make decisions on who would be helped financially or otherwise. Bruce took the ball from Jim and started the process of opening a thrift store in Macomb. When we announced to the church to clean out their closets, basements, and garages and bring it to the church, entire semi trailers were being filled up. We hired our staff out of Celebrate Recovery at minimum wage. We had no idea just how successful the idea would be. Our revenue after expenses increased our benevolence opportunity exponentially. It wasn't long before we opened our second store in Quincy. Both of these stores are generating close to $180,000.00 annually after expenses strictly for benevolence! We employ 14 people from Celebrate Recovery programs in Quincy and Macomb to run the stores. Donations and revenue stream have never slowed down. All shirts are $1, pants are $2, coats are $2, shoes are $1. Furniture, appliances, and house wares are very inexpensive.

Here is what is happening: we are providing a new opportunity for how people can give to the church. We are becoming the community leader in benevolent giving for the poor. We are providing jobs for many people who otherwise might not be able to get back into the work force. We are providing clothes and other needs at an extremely low cost for the needy. Clothes that are not purchased after being on the floor for some time are put in a free bin for whoever wants it. Unclaimed free bin clothes and toys are crated up and sent to our location in South Africa where they are distributed in the townships. Where's the down side? The community now sees the Crossing not only as a cutting-edge church, but also as a heart of compassion in the community.

The Crossing now has a ministry that connects those in need with people from our church that counsel them as to their needs. They do an evaluation that includes virtually every area of their lives. Not only do we help financially, we enroll them in Financial Peace University, get them connected to a small group, and set them up with ongoing counseling. If they have immediate needs, we can send them to the thrift store with a voucher. Our benevolence ministry is interfaced with many gifted people in our congregations. Through this, we can provide services like haircuts or childcare. It is simply the church being the church...

> *"All the believers were together and had everything in common. Selling their possessions and goods, they gave to anyone as he had need. Every day they continued to meet together in the temple courts. They broke bread in their homes and ate together with glad and sincere hearts, praising God and enjoying the favor of all the people. And the Lord added to their number daily those who were being saved."*
>
> *Acts 2:44-47*

The micromissional influence of the Crossing is still growing. It's been amazing to me how quickly God has responded to obstacles in this area and provided whatever we have needed to be the most effective. Recently, Jim came into my office again with another idea. He had driven by an old church building for sale in a much more economically depressed part of the community. He thought it might be a great place to have a resident discipleship program for people desiring to have a stable environment to recover from their addiction. We also saw the facility as another location for Celebrate Recovery meetings, after school programs, VBS, a soup kitchen, and weekend services. The process started moving forward. Celebrate Recovery people went door to door in the neighborhood to let them know what we were thinking. The neighbors liked the idea of a church like the Crossing coming into the neighborhood, but some were very much against the resident program for addiction. We had a neighborhood town hall meeting to discuss their concerns. It was amazing to me how many people there were in the midst of addiction themselves. On the weekend I preached that if God closed the door of this one opportunity, He had something better. When we realized that the city was leaning toward the desires of the disgruntled neighbors, we took the resident program off the table, trusting God to provide.

Three wealthy men stood up and contacted Jim. One wasn't even a member of our church. They said they wanted to fund a project for the resident program. One of them said he had a pre-engineered steel building he had purchased for another project but hadn't constructed. The 8500 square foot building had cost about $80,000.00 but he would be happy to give it to us free of charge. Now we not only have a facility to do benevolence in the middle of the community that needs it, we also have a building that can house more than twice as many men who wish to recover from their addictions. Other business leaders have stepped up to provide them jobs if they need it to get them on their feet.

We are excited not only for the impact from these buildings, but also for the doors that might open with this model into rural communities. We wonder if God has put us in this situation to teach us new ways to use resources to reach into even more areas with the gospel. If we can be satisfied with 500 to 1000 in multi-site campuses inside micropolitan communities with an acquired debt of 1.5 million dollars, could we think about reaching into a rural community with a model that costs a tenth of that with a fourth of the return in people? Benevolence has been an incredible game changer because it is opening our minds up to entirely new ways of accomplishing our vision without worrying about the lid of acquiring huge amounts of debt in the process. The Crossing is impacting the world micromissionally through the establishment of campuses, practicing proactive benevolence, and the pursuit of meaningful and lasting relationships that come by walking through the newly opened doors.

Bibliography

1. Kinnally, Nancy, *Clinton Chooses Quincy as Example of U.S. Economic Recovery*, Great River Development, IDC News 1/2000

2. *Small rural towns get new name-and new attention-Metropolitan and Micropolitan Statistical Area Definitions*, Montana Associated Technology Roundtables, 6/2003

3. Chuang D.J., *Winchester Virginia Becoming Micropolitan*, www.djchuang.com, 2007

4. Nassar, Haya El, *Small Town USA Goes 'Micropolitan'*, Money Magazine, 6/2004

5. Ibid.

6. Pepper, Colleen, *Multiple Everything Insights from Churches with Four or More Campuses*, Leadership Network Article, www.leadnet.org, , 2008

7. Kinneman, David, **Unchristian**: *What a new generation really thinks about Christianity*, Baker Books, 12/2007

8. Scott Thumma and Warren Bird, **Changes in American Megachurches**: *Tracing Eight Years of Growth and*

Innovation in the Nation's Largest Attendance Congregations, Leadership Network and Hartford Seminary, Hartford Institute for Religion Research, 2008.

9. Scott Thumma and Warren Bird, *Not Who You Think They Are: The real story of People who attend America's Megachurches*, www.hartsem.edu, www.leadnet.org, 8/2008.

10. Rowland, Darrel, *The Multisite Phenomenon: Here to Stay?*, Christian Standard, 8/2009.

11. Ibid.

12. Ibid.

13. Ibid.

14. Buford, Bob, *Halftime*, Zondervan, 1994.

Other References:

Scripture taken from the Holy Bible, New International Version.

1. Putman, Jim, ***Church Is A Team Sport***, Baker Books, 2008

2. Henry Blackaby and Claude V. King, ***Experiencing God****: Knowing and Doing the Will of God*, Lifeway Press, 1990.

3. Collins, Jim, ***Good to Great****: Why Some Companies Make the Leap...and Others Don't*, Harper Collins, 2001.

4. Collins, Jim, ***How The Mighty Fall****: And Why Some Companies Never Give In*, Harper Collins, 2009

5. Geoff Surratt, Greg Ligon, Warren Bird, ***The Multi-Site Church Revolution***, Zondervan, 2006

Jerry Harris is the Lead Pastor of The Crossing, a missional, multi-site, megachurch planted in multiple micropolitan communities. The Crossing has grown from 230 people to over 4000 people in communities that aren't growing or even in decline, causing Outreach Magazine to name The Crossing as the 27ᵗʰ fastest growing church in the nation. Receiving his education from Indiana University and Ozark Christian College, Jerry has ministered in Florida, Virginia, Indiana and Illinois. Under his leadership, The Crossing now ministers in 6 locations in Illinois, Missouri, and South Africa. Jerry and his wife Allison have been ministering together for 27 years. They have four children and reside in Quincy, Illinois.

CPSIA information can be obtained at www.ICGtesting.com
Printed in the USA
LVOW052115160912

298962LV00001BA/249/P